THE GREATEST GIFT GIVEN

THE GREATEST GIFT GIVEN

Copyright © 2021 by Love God Greatly Ministry

Permission is granted to print and reproduce this document for the purpose of completing *The Greatest Gift Given* online Bible study. Please do not alter this document in any way. All rights reserved. Published in Dallas by Love God Greatly.

Photo source:
unsplash.com

Recipe source:
Lori, LGG Bengali Branch

Information and data source:
Joshua Project, https://joshuaproject.net/languages/ben, accessed June 2021.

The devotion for Week 6, Tuesday is an excerpt from *Quieting the Shout of Should* by Crystal Stine.

Unless otherwise directed in writing by the Publisher, Scripture quotations are from the NET BIBLE® translation, copyright 2019, by Bible.org. Used by permission. All rights reserved.

Printed in the United States of America, Library of Congress Cataloging-in-Publication Data, Printed in the United States of America

26	25	24	23	22	21
6	5	4	3	2	1

WHEN WOMEN ARE
EQUIPPED WITH THE
KNOWLEDGE OF GOD'S
TRUTH, THE WORLD
IS TRANSFORMED ONE
WOMAN AT A TIME.

JOURNAL BELONGS TO

DATE

CONTENTS

003 WELCOME
005 ABOUT LGG
006 OUR MISSION
008 SOAP BIBLE STUDY METHOD
013 TESTIMONY
014 GLOBAL OUTREACH
016 RECIPE
018 KNOW THESE TRUTHS
023 INTRODUCTION
024 READING PLAN
027 GOALS
029 WEEK 1
057 WEEK 2
085 WEEK 3
113 WEEK 4
141 WEEK 5
169 WEEK 6
197 BRIDGE READING PLAN
199 BRIDGE WEEK 1
229 BRIDGE WEEK 2
257 JOIN US
259 FOR YOU

You
HAVE BEEN
PRAYED FOR;
IT IS NOT A
COINCIDENCE
YOU ARE
PARTICIPATING
IN THIS
STUDY.

WELCOME FRIEND!

We are glad you have decided to join us in this Bible study! You have been prayed for; it is not a coincidence you are participating in this study.

Our prayer for you is simple: that you will grow closer to our Lord as you dig into His Word each and every day. Each day before you read the assigned passage, pray and ask God to help you understand it. Invite Him to speak to you through His Word. Then listen. Believe He will be faithful to speak to you, and be faithful to listen and obey.

Take time to read the verses over and over again. The Bible tells us that if we seek wisdom like silver, and search for it like hidden treasure, then we will understand how to fear the Lord, and we will discover knowledge about God (Prov 2:4-5).

All of us here at Love God Greatly can't wait for you to get started, and we hope to see you at the finish line. Endure, persevere, press on; don't give up! Finish well what you are beginning today.

We will be here every step of the way, cheering for you! We are in this together. Be expectant that God has much in store for you in this study. Journey with us as we learn to love God greatly with our lives!

ABOUT LGG

Love God Greatly exists to inspire, encourage, and equip women around the world to love God greatly with their lives.

INSPIRE women to make God's Word a priority in their daily lives through Bible study resources.

ENCOURAGE women in their walks with God through online community and personal accountability.

EQUIP women to grow in their faith so they can effectively reach others for Christ.

We start with a simple Bible reading plan, but it doesn't stop there. Some women gather in homes and churches locally, while others connect online with women across the globe, Whatever the method, we lovingly lock arms and unite for this purpose: to love God greatly with our lives.

At Love God Greatly, you'll find real, authentic women. You'll find women who desire less of each other, and a whole lot more of Jesus. Women who long to know God through His Word because we believe that truth transforms and sets us free. Women who are better together, saturated in God's Word and in community with one another.

Love God Greatly is committed to providing quality Bible study materials and believes finances should never get in the way of a woman being able to participate in one of our studies. All journals are available to download for free from LoveGodGreatly.com.

Our journals and books are also available for sale on Amazon. Search for "Love God Greatly" to see all of our Bible study journals and books.

YOU'LL FIND WOMEN WHO ARE IMPERFECT, YET FORGIVEN.

Love God Greatly is a 501 (C) (3) non-profit organization. Funding for Love God Greatly comes through donations and proceeds from our online Bible study journals and books.

One-hundred percent of proceeds go directly back into supporting Love God Greatly and helping us inspire, encourage, and equip women all over the world with God's Word.

Arm-in-arm and hand-in-hand, let's do this together.

OUR MISSION

THE NEED

Billions of women around the world don't have access to God's Word in their native language. Those who do, don't have access to women's Bible studies designed and written with them in mind.

THE MISSION

At Love God Greatly, we create Bible studies in 35+ languages. We equip missionaries, ministries, local churches, and women with God's Word at an unprecedented rate by allowing our journals to be downloaded from our international sites at no cost.

Through studying the Bible in their own language with like-minded communities, women are trained and equipped with God's Word.

We believe when women read and apply God's Word to their lives and embrace His unchanging love for them, the world is a better place. We know one woman in God's Word can change a family, a community, and a nation… one woman at a time.

PARTNER WITH US

We would love for you to join us in our mission of giving women all over the world access to God's Word and quality Bible study resources! For any questions or for more information, email us or visit us online. We would love to hear from you!

INFO@LOVEGODGREATLY.COM

LOVEGODGREATLY.COM

AT LOVE GOD GREATLY, WE CREATE BIBLE STUDIES IN 35+ LANGUAGES.

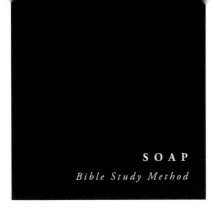

SOAP
Bible Study Method

At Love God Greatly, we believe that the Word of God is living and active. The words of Scripture are powerful and effective and relevant for life in all times and all cultures. In order to interpret the Bible correctly, we need an understanding of the context and culture of the original writings.

As we study the Bible, we use the SOAP Bible Study Method. The acronym stands for Scripture, Observation, Application, and Prayer. It's one thing simply to read Scripture. When you interact with it, intentionally slowing down to reflect, truths start jumping off the page. The SOAP Method allows us to dig deeper into Scripture and see more than we would if we simply read the verses. It allows us not only to be hearers of the Word, but doers as well (Jas 1:22).

YOU WILL NEVER WASTE TIME IN GOD'S WORD. IT IS LIVING, POWERFUL, AND EFFECTIVE, AND HE SPEAKS TO US THROUGH IT.

In this journal, we read a passage of Scripture and then apply the SOAP Method to specific verses. Using this method allows us to glean a greater understanding of Scripture, which allows us to apply it effectively to our lives.

The most important ingredients in the SOAP Method are your interaction with God's Word and your application of it to your life. Take time to study it carefully, discovering the truth of God's character and heart for the world.

Studying God's Word can be challenging and even confusing. We use the SOAP method to help us simplify our study and focus on key passages.

SOAP
Bible Study Method

S
STANDS FOR SCRIPTURE

Physically write out the SOAP verses.

You'll be amazed at what God will reveal to you just by taking the time to slow down and write out what you are reading!

SOAP
WEEK 1 • MONDAY

SCRIPTURE / Write out the SOAP verses

Then I heard a loud voice in heaven saying, "The salvation and the power and the kingdom of our God, and the ruling authority of his Christ, have now come, because the accuser of our brothers and sisters, the one who accuses them day and night before our God, has been thrown down. Revelation 12:10

But the Lord is faithful, and he will strengthen you and protect you from the evil one. 2 Thessalonians 3:3

OBSERVATION / Write 3-4 observations

Loud voice, powerful, all knowing
We are accused day and night, constant struggle
The Lord will help, establish and guard me
He's always there
He's is constant, a protector in my life, guardian

O
STANDS FOR OBSERVATION

What do you see in the verses that you're reading?

Who is the intended audience? Is there a repetition of words?

What words stand out to you?

A
STANDS FOR APPLICATION

This is when God's Word becomes personal.

What is God saying to you today? How can you apply what you just read to your own personal life?

What changes do you need to make? Is there action you need to take?

P
STANDS FOR PRAYER

Pray God's Word back to Him.
Spend time thanking Him.

If He has revealed something to you during this time in His Word, pray about it.

If He has revealed some sin that is in your life, confess. And remember, He loves you dearly.

APPLICATION / *Write down 1 - 2 applications*

Remind myself of God's strength is more powerful than anything
Memorize these verses and say them daily this week
Ask God to strengthen my faith in Him
Trust God that he will deliver me from evil
Pray for my brothers and sisters in Christ

PRAYER / *Write out a prayer over what you learned*

Dear Lord,

Thank you for being constant, faithful, and loving towards me and my life. Help me to further my trust and faith in you daily and through difficult times.

Help me to know you're alway there by my side, guarding, and protecting me. Remind me of the suffering of others and to be able to help and encourage them in their growth.

I ask all these things in Jesus name.
Amen

LANGUAGE HIGHLIGHT

TESTIMONY

LGG Bengali Branch

After I came to the Lord, God placed a desire for missions in me, though it didn't happen right away. I didn't realize that God was always working toward this in my life, even though things both within and beyond my control caused many delays. I made a lot of international friends and I prayed often for different parts of the world. But I still waited for God to give me a specific international mission field.

Finally, God connected me with a man from Bangladesh. He was a former Muslim who had been following Christ for about ten years. He was rejected by many, including his parents. He had done training and evangelism through an organization called Cru and was active in many universities and colleges in Bangladesh. I was deeply moved by His passion for serving the Lord. We began to pray together and do Bible studies together through social media. As we did, we began to care deeply for each other and knew that we should serve God together, as the Lord had divinely shown us!

By steps of faith, I came to Bangladesh and we were married! Now we live to serve the Lord, here together in Bangladesh for the Lord's glory! Praise God for His leading and all His precious promises to us!

PRAISE GOD FOR HIS LEADING AND ALL HIS PRECIOUS PROMISES TO US!

God led me to Love God Greatly through the YouVersion Bible devotionals. I discovered that these studies were translated into over 35 languages, and was thrilled! This was great news! I now serve with the Love God Greatly Bengali team, making these studies available in the Bengali language, where they are so desperately needed!

We pray that many women in Bangladesh will find a new passion and love for God and His Word through studying the Bible!

LGG Bengali Branch

LANGUAGE	GLOBAL SPEAKERS	TO CONNECT WITH THIS BRANCH
Bengali	225,295,000	Email: lggbengali@gmail.com

LGG HOME

Do you know someone who could use our Love God Greatly Bible studies in the Bengali language?

If so, make sure and tell them all the amazing Bible study resources we provide to help equip them with God's Word!

LANGUAGE HIGHLIGHT
GLOBAL OUTREACH
LGG Bengali Branch

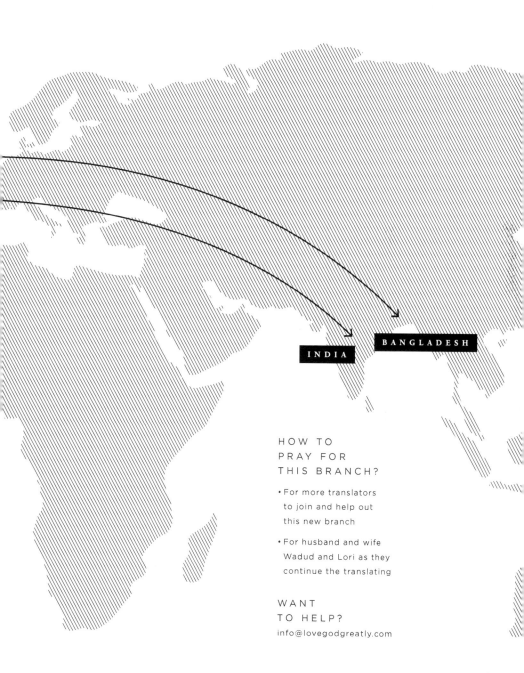

INDIA

BANGLADESH

HOW TO PRAY FOR THIS BRANCH?

- For more translators to join and help out this new branch
- For husband and wife Wadud and Lori as they continue the translating

WANT TO HELP?
info@lovegodgreatly.com

LANGUAGE HIGHLIGHT

RECIPE

LGG Bengali Branch

Mung Dal

(Serves 4 to 6+)

INGREDIENTS

1 CUP DRY MUNG DAL
(Split Mung Beans)

3 SMALL SIZE BABY ONIONS

1 HEAD OF GARLIC

1 SMALL PIECE OF WHOLE GINGER

3 TSP TURMERIC

2 TSP SALT

2 TSP COOKING OIL

1-2 TSP PONCH PARAN
(Bengali Five-Spice)

DIRECTIONS

Cover the Mung Dal generously with water and soak for 10-15 minutes. Then, rinse and drain the water, and place the Mung Dal in a medium or large pot.

Chop 2 onions. Separate, peel, and chop the garlic cloves in half. Add onions and garlic to the pot along with ginger, turmeric, salt, and oil. Pour in 6 cups of water and bring to a boil. After reaching a boil, reduce the heat and simmer for 40 minutes, or until Dal is soft and can be mashed easily. Pull Mung Dal out of the pot and mash. Return to pot and add another 4 cups of water. Bring to boil for another 3-4 minutes, and set aside.

Fry Ponch Paran with 2 tsp of chopped onion and add to Mung Dal. Stir, bring to boil another 3-5 minutes, cool, and serve.

KNOW THESE TRUTHS

GOD LOVES YOU

God's Word says, "For this is the way God loved the world: He gave his one and only Son, so that everyone who believes in him will not perish but have eternal life" (John 3:16).

OUR SIN SEPARATES US FROM GOD

We are all sinners by nature and by choice, and because of this we are separated from God, who is holy. God's Word says, "for all have sinned and fall short of the glory of God" (Rom 3:23).

JESUS DIED SO YOU MIGHT HAVE LIFE

The consequence of sin is death, but God's free gift of salvation is available to us. Jesus took the penalty for our sin when He died on the cross.

God's Word says, "For the payoff of sin is death, but the gift of God is eternal life in Christ Jesus our Lord" (Rom 6:23); "But God demonstrates his own love for us, in that while we were still sinners, Christ died for us" (Rom 5:8).

JESUS LIVES!

Death could not hold Him, and three days after His body was placed in the tomb Jesus rose again, defeating sin and death forever. He lives today in heaven and is preparing a place in eternity for all who believe in Him.

Jesus says, "There are many dwelling places in my Father's house. Otherwise, I would have told you, because I am going away to make ready a place for you. And if I go and make ready a place for you, I will come again and take you to be with me, so that where I am you may be too" (John 14:2–3).

KNOW YOU CAN BE FORGIVEN

Accepting Jesus as your Savior is not about what you can do, but rather about having faith in what Jesus has already done. It takes recognizing that you are a sinner, believing that Jesus died for your sins, and asking for forgiveness by placing your full trust in Jesus' work on the cross on your behalf.

God's Word says, "if you confess with your mouth that Jesus is Lord and believe in your heart that God raised him from the dead, you will be saved. For with the heart one believes and thus has righteousness and with the mouth one confesses and thus has salvation" (Rom 10:9–10).

ACCEPT CHRIST'S FREE GIFT OF SALVATION

Practically, what does that look like? With a sincere heart, you can pray a simple prayer like this:

Jesus,
I know that I am a sinner. I don't want to live another day without embracing the love and forgiveness that You have for me. I ask for Your forgiveness. I believe that You died for my sins and rose from the dead. I surrender all that I am and ask You to be Lord of my life. Help me to turn from my sin and follow You. Teach me what it means to walk in freedom as I live under Your grace, and help me to grow in Your ways as I seek to know You more. Amen.

CONNECT AND GROW

If you just prayed this prayer (or something similar in your own words) we'd love to connect with you!

You can email us at info@lovegodgreatly.com. We'd love to celebrate with you, pray with you, and help you connect to a local church. We are here to encourage you as you begin your new life as a child of God.

Let's Begin

THE GREATEST GIFT GIVEN

Introduction

When we receive an anonymous gift, it may be exciting and enjoyable, but it lacks an understanding of why the gift was given. When our best friend gives us a gift, we know it was done out of love for us, knowledge of us, and care for us. Gifts have meaning because of the giver.

GOD IS THE ONE WHO GIVES US EVERY PERFECT GIFT.

God is the One who gives us every perfect gift. Not only did He give us Jesus, His only Son, as the greatest Gift in history, but He continues to offer us gifts every day. He is goodness Himself, withholding nothing good from us because He alone is good. Jesus Christ is the greatest Gift given by the only good Giver, but He is not the only gift God has given us!

HOPE. God promises that our hope, when placed in Jesus, will never disappoint us. We have hope in the promises God gives us and hope in our coming salvation. We can praise God for the gift of hope because, in it, we see His faithfulness.

FAITH. Faith serves a purpose, and without it we cannot please God. But faith is a gift, given to us through Jesus. Through faith, the Holy Spirit works in us to make us more like Christ and to protect us from the attacks of the enemy.

JOY. Apart from Christ, we can never have true, lasting joy. He alone is the source of joy, and He gives us joy each day as we walk with Him. Through Christ alone can we have joy no matter our circumstances.

PEACE. Jesus Christ is the Prince of Peace. In Him we have peace in our hearts and minds because He has won every battle. He goes before us and will never leave us.

As we cling to the Giver and the gifts He gives us, we can live a life of true gratitude to Him. As we study the incredible gifts we have in Christ, we can worship God and praise Him for who He is and what He has done. He is the only Gift we need, and He is the greatest Gift we have been, and ever will be, given.

READING PLAN

WEEK 1: THE GIVER

- *Monday: Goodness Himself*
  Read: Psalm 34:8; Psalm 84; Mark 10:18
  SOAP: Psalm 84:11

- *Tuesday: The Gift of God*
  Read: John 3:16; Romans 6:23; Ephesians 2:8
  SOAP: Ephesians 2:8

- *Wednesday: Every Perfect Gift*
  Read: Luke 11:1–13; James 1:17
  SOAP: James 1:17

- *Thursday: Using Your Gifts*
  Read: 1 Corinthians 12; 1 Peter 4:10–11
  SOAP: 1 Peter 4:10–11

- *Friday: God's Love Endures*
  Read: Psalm 136
  SOAP: Psalm 136:26

WEEK 2: A LIFE OF GRATITUDE

- *Monday: Give Thanks to the Lord*
  Read: Psalm 107
  SOAP: Psalm 107:21–22

- *Tuesday: Gratitude for Gifts*
  Read: Philippians 4:10–20
  SOAP: Philippians 4:18–19

- *Wednesday: Giving from Gratitude*
  Read: Luke 6:37–38; 2 Corinthians 9
  SOAP: 2 Corinthians 9:7–8

- *Thursday: Giving Thanks in All Circumstances*
  Read: Ephesians 5:15–20; 1 Thessalonians 5:16–18
  SOAP: 1 Thessalonians 5:16–18

- *Friday: The Lord is Good*
  Read: Psalm 100
  SOAP: Psalm 100:1–5

WEEK 3: THE GIFT OF HOPE

- ○ *Monday: Hope in God's Love*
  Read: Romans 5:1–11
  SOAP: Romans 5:3–5

- ○ *Tuesday: Hope in the Promise*
  Read: Hebrews 10:19–25
  SOAP: Hebrews 10:23

- ○ *Wednesday: Hope in Christ*
  Read: Romans 15:7–13
  SOAP: Romans 15:13

- ○ *Thursday: Hope in Salvation*
  Read: Romans 8:18–25
  SOAP: Romans 8:24–25

- ○ *Friday: Praise for His Faithfulness*
  Read: Psalm 105
  SOAP: Psalm 105:42–43

WEEK 4: THE GIFT OF FAITH

- ○ *Monday: The Purpose of Faith*
  Read: Hebrews 11
  SOAP: Hebrews 11:1, 6

- ○ *Tuesday: The Promise of Faith*
  Read: Matthew 17:14–20; 21:18–22
  SOAP: Matthew 21:21–22

- ○ *Wednesday: The Result of Faith*
  Read: Matthew 15:21–28; Luke 8:42–48
  SOAP: Matthew 15:28; Luke 8:48

- ○ *Thursday: The Protection of Faith*
  Read: Ephesians 6:10–20
  SOAP: Ephesians 6:16

- ○ *Friday: Praise for His Patience*
  Read: Psalm 103
  SOAP: Psalm 103:8–10

READING PLAN

WEEK 5: THE GIFT OF JOY

- *Monday: Joy in His Presence*
  Read: Psalm 16
  SOAP: Psalm 16:11

- *Tuesday: Joy in Trials*
  Read: Philippians 1; James 1:2–4
  SOAP: James 1:2–4

- *Wednesday: Joy in Worship*
  Read: Psalm 30
  SOAP: Psalm 30:11–12

- *Thursday: Joy in the Promise*
  Read: John 16:19–24
  SOAP: John 16:22

- *Friday: Praise Psalm of Joy*
  Read: Psalm 147
  SOAP: Psalm 147:1

WEEK 6: THE GIFT OF PEACE

- *Monday: Peace in Your Heart*
  Read: Colossians 3:12–17
  SOAP: Colossians 3:15

- *Tuesday: Peace in Your Mind*
  Read: Philippians 4:2–9
  SOAP: Philippians 4:6–8

- *Wednesday: Peace in Your Circumstances*
  Read: Isaiah 26:3; 2 Corinthians 1:3–11
  SOAP: Isaiah 26:3

- *Thursday: Peace in Your Future*
  Read: Isaiah 9:6; John 14:27–31
  SOAP: John 14:27

- *Friday: Praise the Lord!*
  Read: Psalm 113; Luke 1:46–55
  SOAP: Psalm 113:1–2

YOUR GOALS

Write three goals you would like to focus on as you begin each day and dig into God's Word. Make sure you refer back to these goals throughout the next weeks to help you stay focused. You can do it!

ONE

TWO

THREE

WEEK 1

All generous giving and every perfect gift is from above, coming down from the Father of lights, with whom there is no variation or the slightest hint of change.

James 1:17

PRAY

Write down your prayer requests and praises for this week.

WEEKLY CHALLENGE

This week, create a running list of the gifts God has given you. Keep in mind, some of these gifts may not be what you expect. Praise Him for each one of these gifts.

WEEK 1
Monday

READ

Psalm 34:8

Taste and see that the LORD is good. How blessed is the one who takes shelter in him.

Psalm 84
For the music director, according to the gittith *style; written by the Korahites, a psalm.*

How lovely is the place where you live, O LORD of Heaven's Armies! 2 I desperately want to be in the courts of the LORD's temple. My heart and my entire being shout for joy to the living God. 3 Even the birds find a home there, and the swallow builds a nest, where she can protect her young near your altars, O LORD of Heaven's Armies, my King and my God. 4 How blessed are those who live in your temple and praise you continually. (Selah) 5 How blessed are those who find their strength in you, and long to travel the roads that lead to your temple. 6 As they pass through the Baca Valley, he provides a spring for them. The rain even covers it with pools of water. 7 They are sustained as they travel along; each one appears before God in Zion. 8 O LORD God of Heaven's Armies, hear my prayer. Listen, O God of Jacob. (Selah) 9 O God, take notice of our shield. Show concern for your chosen king. 10 Certainly spending just one day in your temple courts is better than spending a thousand elsewhere. I would rather stand at the entrance to the temple of my God than live in the tents of the wicked. 11 For the LORD God is our sovereign protector. The LORD bestows favor and honor; he withholds no good thing from those who have integrity. 12 O LORD of Heaven's Armies, how blessed are those who trust in you.

Mark 10:18

Jesus said to him, "Why do you call me good? No one is good except God alone.

SOAP

WEEK 1 • MONDAY

SOAP / *Psalm 84:11*
SCRIPTURE / *Write out the SOAP verses*

OBSERVATION / *Write 3 - 4 observations*

APPLICATION / *Write down 1 - 2 applications*

PRAYER / *Write out a prayer over what you learned*

DEVOTIONAL
WEEK 1 • MONDAY

SOAP

Psalm 84:11

For the Lord God is our sovereign protector. The Lord bestows favor and honor; he withholds no good thing from those who have integrity.

INTO THE TEXT

Have you ever received an absolutely perfect gift? It was exactly what you hoped for, hinted about, dreamed of, and now it was yours. Maybe it came beautifully wrapped and presented in a way that made you know that, without a doubt, this was special. What made it even better was that the person giving it to you had taken the time to pay attention to what you wanted. They knew what you loved and they made sacrifices of time and money to make sure you received that gift. Receiving that gift made you feel seen and known and loved and valued.

Although the gifts God gives us aren't wrapped up with bows and beautiful paper, they are worth so much more than anything we will ever find under the Christmas tree. God's gifts for us are not simply things that we want, but the soul-satisfying, eternal, loving gifts that God knows we need.

God's gifts to His children are good, because He is goodness. Psalm 34:8 instructs us to "taste and see that the Lord is good," and in Mark 10:18, Jesus tells us that "No one is good except God alone." As we spend time this Advent season unwrapping the good gifts the Father has for us, may our hearts be open to receiving gifts that are so much more than what we want, but exactly what we need.

PRAYER

Father God, You alone are good and I am so honored to receive the good and perfect gifts that You know we need. Thank You for being my protector, my shelter, and my strength. May my entire being shout for joy as I share You—my greatest gift—with those around me. Amen.

WEEK 1
Tuesday

READ

John 3:16

For this is the way God loved the world: He gave his one and only Son, so that everyone who believes in him will not perish but have eternal life.

Romans 6:23

For the payoff of sin is death, but the gift of God is eternal life in Christ Jesus our Lord.

Ephesians 2:8

For by grace you are saved through faith, and this is not from yourselves, it is the gift of God

SOAP

WEEK 1 • TUESDAY

SOAP / *Ephesians 2:8*
SCRIPTURE / *Write out the SOAP verses*

OBSERVATION / *Write 3 - 4 observations*

APPLICATION / *Write down 1 - 2 applications*

PRAYER / *Write out a prayer over what you learned*

DEVOTIONAL
WEEK 1 • TUESDAY

SOAP

Ephesians 2:8

For by grace you are saved through faith, and this is not from yourselves, it is the gift of God.

INTO THE TEXT

Each summer we spend a few weeks going through our home to collect unused or unwanted items to donate or add to a yard sale. There are shoes that no longer fit, cups that lost their lid long ago, that gift from a great-aunt that was very clearly a re-gift and taking up space in our garage. And, inevitably, we add a few things to the pile that, just a few months ago, were on our "must have" list for birthdays or Christmas.

The item was exactly what we thought we wanted, but the reality of it wasn't as perfect as we'd hoped. The toy was fun for a few minutes but was quickly replaced by something else. The appliance we thought we had to have only took up too much room in our cabinets and was harder to use than we ever thought. Things that held enormous value and potential just never quite lived up to our expectations, and now they were in a pile to find a new home.

No gift we could ever receive on this earth will last forever. It will become worn, run out of batteries, break, or be replaced by something new and exciting. That doesn't mean we shouldn't buy gifts for those we love or be excited to receive a gift (it's one of my top love languages), but it does help remind us to put our expectations into perspective.

The greatest gift we could ever receive will never fail us or fade away. The gift of God for all people is salvation through His Son, Jesus Christ. It is freely given, available for everyone, and offers us a place with God for eternity. In this Advent season, how can you share this gift with someone?

PRAYER

God, thank You for the greatest gift You could ever offer me—the gift of salvation through Your Son. Help me see the people in my life who don't yet know about this gift, and open opportunities for me to share the joy I have in You, with them. Amen.

WEEK 1
Wednesday

READ

Luke 11:1–13

Now Jesus was praying in a certain place. When he stopped, one of his disciples said to him, "Lord, teach us to pray, just as John taught his disciples." 2 So he said to them, "When you pray, say: Father, may your name be honored; may your kingdom come. 3 Give us each day our daily bread, 4 and forgive us our sins, for we also forgive everyone who sins against us. And do not lead us into temptation." 5 Then he said to them, "Suppose one of you has a friend, and you go to him at midnight and say to him, 'Friend, lend me three loaves of bread, 6 because a friend of mine has stopped here while on a journey, and I have nothing to set before him.' 7 Then he will reply from inside, 'Do not bother me. The door is already shut, and my children and I are in bed. I cannot get up and give you anything.' 8 I tell you, even though the man inside will not get up and give him anything because he is his friend, yet because of the first man's sheer persistence he will get up and give him whatever he needs. 9 "So I tell you: Ask, and it will be given to you; seek, and you will find; knock, and the door will be opened for you. 10 For everyone who asks receives, and the one who seeks finds, and to the one who knocks, the door will be opened. 11 What father among you, if your son asks for a fish, will give him a snake instead of a fish? 12 Or if he asks for an egg, will give him a scorpion? 13 If you then, although you are evil, know how to give good gifts to your children, how much more will the heavenly Father give the Holy Spirit to those who ask him!"

James 1:17

All generous giving and every perfect gift is from above, coming down from the Father of lights, with whom there is no variation or the slightest hint of change.

SOAP

WEEK 1 • WEDNESDAY

SOAP / *James 1:17*
SCRIPTURE / *Write out the SOAP verses*

OBSERVATION / *Write 3 - 4 observations*

APPLICATION / *Write down 1 - 2 applications*

PRAYER / *Write out a prayer over what you learned*

DEVOTIONAL
WEEK 1 • WEDNESDAY

SOAP

James 1:17

All generous giving and every perfect gift is from above, coming down from the Father of lights, with whom there is no variation or the slightest hint of change.

INTO THE TEXT

In our reading today, both Jesus and James encourage us to go before God with our deepest needs, believing that He will respond with good and perfect gifts because God is good, and His character does not change when our circumstances change.

The early Christian church that James was writing to had been scattered because of persecution. In his letter, he reminded them that clinging tightly to their faith through all kinds of trials would produce in them endurance. For those who asked God for wisdom, they were to ask with confidence, with faith that did not waver or doubt.

In Luke we read that Jesus' disciples asked Him to teach them how to pray. Jesus not only offers a model of prayer, but a glimpse into the nature and character of God. Jesus told us to "ask and it will be given to you; seek, and you will find; knock, and the door will be opened for you" (Luke 11:9). Our Father God loves His children and, although He already knows everything about us, wants us to come into His presence and ask for gifts that align with His will and will advance His kingdom.

If your prayers haven't been answered the way you wanted, trust and believe that our God can only give gifts that align with His character—and He is good. He wants the best for you. James calls God "the Father of lights," and in this Advent season may each Christmas light you see remind you that God's ways are better than your ways, He is unchanging, and He loves you so much that He cannot give you anything but the best—even when it's not what you expected.

PRAYER

Father God, thank You for inviting me to come to You in prayer with the deepest desires of my heart, the places I feel weak and powerless and in need of Your provision. As I hang Christmas lights or see them on my neighbor's homes, may I be reminded that all good and perfect gifts come from You, and that You love me. Amen.

WEEK 1
Thursday

READ

1 Corinthians 12

With regard to spiritual gifts, brothers and sisters, I do not want you to be uninformed. 2 You know that when you were pagans you were often led astray by speechless idols, however you were led. 3 So I want you to understand that no one speaking by the Spirit of God says, "Jesus is cursed," and no one can say, "Jesus is Lord," except by the Holy Spirit. 4 Now there are different gifts, but the same Spirit. 5 And there are different ministries, but the same Lord. 6 And there are different results, but the same God who produces all of them in everyone. 7 To each person the manifestation of the Spirit is given for the benefit of all. 8 For one person is given through the Spirit the message of wisdom, and another the message of knowledge according to the same Spirit, 9 to another faith by the same Spirit, and to another gifts of healing by the one Spirit, 10 to another performance of miracles, to another prophecy, and to another discernment of spirits, to another different kinds of tongues, and to another the interpretation of tongues. 11 It is one and the same Spirit, distributing as he decides to each person, who produces all these things. 12 For just as the body is one and yet has many members, and all the members of the body—though many—are one body, so too is Christ. 13 For in one Spirit we were all baptized into one body. Whether Jews or Greeks or slaves or free, we were all made to drink of the one Spirit. 14 For in fact the body is not a single member, but many. 15 If the foot says, "Since I am not a hand, I am not part of the body," it does not lose its membership in the body because of that. 16 And if the ear says, "Since I am not an eye, I am not part of the body," it does not lose its membership in the body because of that. 17 If the whole body were an eye, what part would do the hearing? If the whole were an ear, what

WEEK 1
Thursday

1 Corinthians 12 (continued)

part would exercise the sense of smell? 18 But as a matter of fact, God has placed each of the members in the body just as he decided. 19 If they were all the same member, where would the body be? 20 So now there are many members, but one body. 21 The eye cannot say to the hand, "I do not need you," nor in turn can the head say to the foot, "I do not need you." 22 On the contrary, those members that seem to be weaker are essential, 23 and those members we consider less honorable we clothe with greater honor, and our unpresentable members are clothed with dignity, 24 but our presentable members do not need this. Instead, God has blended together the body, giving greater honor to the lesser member, 25 so that there may be no division in the body, but the members may have mutual concern for one another. 26 If one member suffers, everyone suffers with it. If a member is honored, all rejoice with it. 27 Now you are Christ's body, and each of you is a member of it. 28 And God has placed in the church first apostles, second prophets, third teachers, then miracles, gifts of healing, helps, gifts of leadership, different kinds of tongues. 29 Not all are apostles, are they? Not all are prophets, are they? Not all are teachers, are they? Not all perform miracles, do they? 30 Not all have gifts of healing, do they? Not all speak in tongues, do they? Not all interpret, do they? 31 But you should be eager for the greater gifts. And now I will show you a way that is beyond comparison.

1 Peter 4:10–11

Just as each one has received a gift, use it to serve one another as good stewards of the varied grace of God. 11 Whoever speaks, let it be with God's words. Whoever serves, do so with the strength that God supplies, so that in everything God will be glorified through Jesus Christ. To him belong the glory and the power forever and ever. Amen.

"May God give you peace with yourselves; may he give you good will towards all your friends, your enemies, and your neighbors; and may he give you grace to give glory to God in the highest."

Charles Spurgeon

SOAP

WEEK 1 • THURSDAY

SOAP / *1 Peter 4:10–11*
SCRIPTURE / *Write out the SOAP verses*

OBSERVATION / *Write 3 - 4 observations*

APPLICATION / *Write down 1 - 2 applications*

PRAYER / *Write out a prayer over what you learned*

DEVOTIONAL
WEEK 1 • THURSDAY

SOAP

1 Peter 4:10–11

Just as each one has received a gift, use it to serve one another as good stewards of the varied grace of God. Whoever speaks, let it be with God's words. Whoever serves, do so with the strength that God supplies, so that in everything God will be glorified through Jesus Christ. To him belong the glory and the power forever and ever. Amen.

INTO THE TEXT

What happens on Christmas morning when siblings or cousins gather together to open gifts? Sometimes it's pure chaos, and no one ever really knows what the others received until the bows and wrapping paper have finally settled to the ground. Or if your family gatherings are a little more organized, each child unwraps one gift at a time so everyone has a chance to be in the spotlight. Inevitably, no matter how the gifts are opened, there will be a moment of comparison. How does what I received compare to what they just opened? Would I rather have something different, or am I content with what I've been given?

The gifts our good God gives us are not items to unwrap under the Christmas tree, but elements of our personality and character that make us uniquely designed to advance His kingdom. The gifts believers receive from the Holy Spirit are intended to be used together to create unity, not set us apart from one another. All of these gifts: wisdom, knowledge, faith, healing, miracles, prophesy, discernment—they're all meant to be better together.

When we embrace the gifts God has given us and use them for His glory and not our own, our families, communities, and churches benefit. Although you might look side-to-side to see what someone else has received, believe that God designed you in a beautiful way to be uniquely equipped to use your gift for His glory. Look around, but only to see where your gift can encourage someone else. Look around, but only to see where you can collaborate instead of compare. But most of all, look up, thanking God for giving you an amazing gift.

PRAYER

God, it can be easy for us to look at other believers and compare gifts and opportunities. Help us to stay focused right where You have called us, serving You and not our own agendas. May we commit to using our gifts to grow Your kingdom and bring You glory, because we are truly better together. Amen.

WEEK 1
Friday

READ

Psalm 136

Give thanks to the Lord, for he is good, for his loyal love endures. 2 Give thanks to the God of gods, for his loyal love endures. 3 Give thanks to the Lord of lords, for his loyal love endures, 4 to the one who performs magnificent, amazing deeds all by himself, for his loyal love endures, 5 to the one who used wisdom to make the heavens, for his loyal love endures, 6 to the one who spread out the earth over the water, for his loyal love endures, 7 to the one who made the great lights, for his loyal love endures, 8 the sun to rule by day, for his loyal love endures, 9 the moon and stars to rule by night, for his loyal love endures, 10 to the one who struck down the firstborn of Egypt, for his loyal love endures, 11 and led Israel out from their midst, for his loyal love endures, 12 with a strong hand and an outstretched arm, for his loyal love endures, 13 to the one who divided the Red Sea in two, for his loyal love endures, 14 and led Israel through its midst, for his loyal love endures, 15 and tossed Pharaoh and his army into the Red Sea, for his loyal love endures, 16 to the one who led his people through the wilderness, for his loyal love endures, 17 to the one who struck down great kings, for his loyal love endures, 18 and killed powerful kings, for his loyal love endures, 19 Sihon, king of the Amorites, for his loyal love endures, 20 Og, king of Bashan, for his loyal love endures, 21 and gave their land as an inheritance, for his loyal love endures, 22 as an inheritance to Israel his servant, for his loyal love endures, 23 to the one who remembered us when we were down, for his loyal love endures, 24 and snatched us away from our enemies, for his loyal love endures, 25 to the one who gives food to all living things, for his loyal love endures. 26 Give thanks to the God of heaven, for his loyal love endures!

SOAP

WEEK 1 • FRIDAY

SOAP / *Psalm 136:26*
SCRIPTURE / *Write out the SOAP verses*

OBSERVATION / *Write 3 - 4 observations*

APPLICATION / *Write down 1 - 2 applications*

PRAYER / *Write out a prayer over what you learned*

DEVOTIONAL
WEEK 1 • FRIDAY

SOAP

Psalm 136:26

Give thanks to the God of heaven, for his loyal love endures!

INTO THE TEXT

There is something special about receiving a "thank you" note in the mail. After you've put the time, effort, and resources into doing something special for someone else, a handwritten note or a text message that says "thank you" feels like a gift in return. It's not often something we need, because we love making our loved ones feel special, but it's a blessing of thoughtfulness.

Reading through Psalm 136 today gives us twenty-six reasons to give thanks to the Lord! Our relationship with God is more than us asking for gifts and God responding. It's using our gifts to honor and glorify God, remembering all that He has done for us, worshipping Him for who He is and what He has done, celebrating His unchanging character, telling others about Him and the gift of salvation He has for each of us, and giving Him thanks with joyful hearts.

When was the last time you used your time with God to just say "thank you"? Thank Him for who He is—our good God, the Lord of lords, the King of kings. Thank Him for what He has done—what He has created, the gifts He has given you, the prayers He has answered. Remember the times God closed doors, made a way, offered protection, stood firm as your refuge, and comforted you. Thank God for loving you when you were still a sinner, for calling you His daughter, for making a place and a way for you to live with Him for eternity. Thank God for sending His Son to earth to be the greatest gift you could ever receive.

Give thanks to the Lord!

PRAYER

God, today I come humbly before You in thanksgiving, not to ask for anything but to remember and celebrate all that You have already done, all that You are, and all that You have given so freely to me. I love You. Amen.

REFLECT
WEEK 1

1. How do you find comfort knowing God is your protector?

   ....
   ....
   ....

2. Do you believe that God does not withhold anything good from you? How do you reconcile this truth when God does not answer your prayers in the way you hoped?

   ....
   ....
   ....

3. How is salvation a gift from God?

   ....
   ....
   ....

4. What are some of the spiritual gifts God has given you? How can you use these gifts to bless the body of Christ?

   ....
   ....
   ....

5. How can you give thanks to God for His love today?

   ....
   ....
   ....

JOURNAL
your thoughts

JOURNAL
your thoughts

WEEK 2

Always *rejoice*
constantly *pray*
in *everything*
give thanks.
For this is God's
will for you in
Christ Jesus.

1 Thessalonians 5:16-18

PRAY

Write down your prayer requests and praises for this week.

WEEKLY CHALLENGE

Focus on 1 Thessalonians 5:16–18 this week. How can you always rejoice? What does it mean to constantly pray? Are you willing to give thanks in everything, even hardship and disappointment? Reflect on what God teaches you.

WEEK 2

Monday

READ

Psalm 107

Give thanks to the LORD, for he is good, and his loyal love endures. 2 Let those delivered by the LORD speak out, those whom he delivered from the power of the enemy, 3 and gathered from foreign lands, from east and west, from north and south. 4 They wandered through the wilderness, in a wasteland; they found no road to a city in which to live. 5 They were hungry and thirsty; they fainted from exhaustion. 6 They cried out to the LORD in their distress; he delivered them from their troubles. 7 He led them on a level road, that they might find a city in which to live. 8 Let them give thanks to the LORD for his loyal love, and for the amazing things he has done for people. 9 For he has satisfied those who thirst, and those who hunger he has filled with food. 10 They sat in utter darkness, bound in painful iron chains, 11 because they had rebelled against God's commands, and rejected the instructions of the Most High. 12 So he used suffering to humble them; they stumbled and no one helped them up. 13 They cried out to the LORD in their distress; he delivered them from their troubles. 14 He brought them out of the utter darkness, and tore off their shackles. 15 Let them give thanks to the LORD for his loyal love, and for the amazing things he has done for people. 16 For he shattered the bronze gates, and hacked through the iron bars. 17 They acted like fools in their rebellious ways, and suffered because of their sins. 18 They lost their appetite for all food, and they drew near the gates of death. 19 They cried out to the LORD in their distress; he delivered them from their troubles. 20 He sent them an assuring word and healed them; he rescued them from the pits where they were trapped. 21 Let them give thanks to the LORD for his loyal love, and for the amazing things he has done for people. 22 Let them

WEEK 2

Monday

Psalm 107 (continued)

present thank offerings, and loudly proclaim what he has done. 23 Some traveled on the sea in ships, and carried cargo over the vast waters. 24 They witnessed the acts of the Lord, his amazing feats on the deep water. 25 He gave the order for a windstorm, and it stirred up the waves of the sea. 26 They reached up to the sky, then dropped into the depths. The sailors' strength left them because the danger was so great. 27 They swayed and staggered like drunks, and all their skill proved ineffective. 28 They cried out to the Lord in their distress; he delivered them from their troubles. 29 He calmed the storm, and the waves grew silent. 30 The sailors rejoiced because the waves grew quiet, and he led them to the harbor they desired. 31 Let them give thanks to the Lord for his loyal love, and for the amazing things he has done for people. 32 Let them exalt him in the assembly of the people. Let them praise him in the place where the leaders preside. 33 He turned streams into a desert, springs of water into arid land, 34 and a fruitful land into a barren place, because of the sin of its inhabitants. 35 As for his people, he turned a desert into a pool of water, and a dry land into springs of water. 36 He allowed the hungry to settle there, and they established a city in which to live. 37 They cultivated fields, and planted vineyards, which yielded a harvest of fruit. 38 He blessed them so that they became very numerous. He would not allow their cattle to decrease in number. 39 As for their enemies, they decreased in number and were beaten down, because of painful distress and suffering. 40 He would pour contempt upon princes, and he made them wander in a wasteland with no road. 41 Yet he protected the needy from oppression, and cared for his families like a flock of sheep. 42 When the godly see this, they rejoice, and every sinner shuts his mouth. 43 Whoever is wise, let him take note of these things. Let them consider the Lord's acts of loyal love.

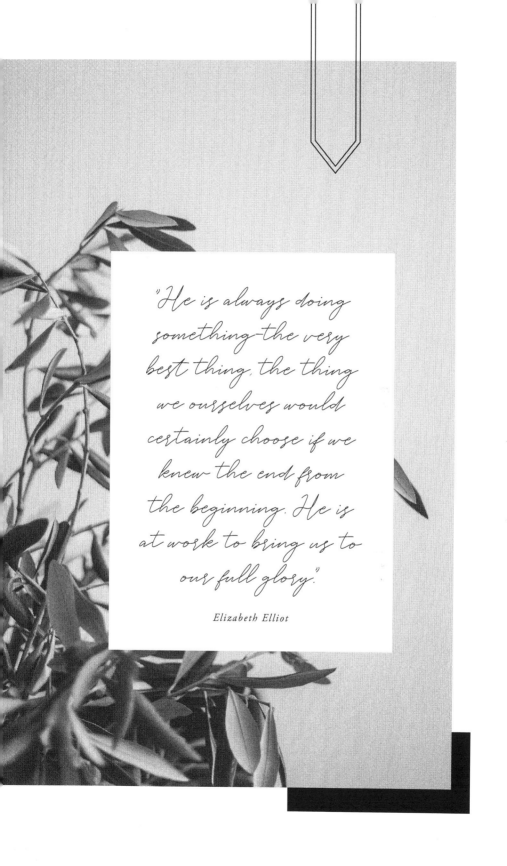

"He is always doing something—the very best thing, the thing we ourselves would certainly choose if we knew the end from the beginning. He is at work to bring us to our full glory."

Elizabeth Elliot

SOAP

WEEK 2 • MONDAY

SOAP / *Psalm 107:21–22*
SCRIPTURE / *Write out the SOAP verses*

OBSERVATION / *Write 3 - 4 observations*

APPLICATION / *Write down 1 - 2 applications*

PRAYER / *Write out a prayer over what you learned*

DEVOTIONAL
WEEK 2 • MONDAY

SOAP

Psalm 107:21–22

Let them give thanks to the Lord for his loyal love, and for the amazing things he has done for people. Let them present thank offerings, and loudly proclaim what he has done.

INTO THE TEXT

Do you find yourself entering this season with a weary heart, feeling like you've been wandering, exhausted, in distress, troubled, and looking for a light in the darkness? The world around you might be bustling with joy and excitement, but you're looking for a place of refuge to rest and recover from the weight of all that you've carried this year.

God understands, and He invites you to come into His perfect rest. Your weariness and frustration is not new to Him, and He will not be surprised by your very honest feelings and heartache. Read our Scripture passage today and enter your name everywhere it says "those" or "them." The same way God delivered and provided for those who wandered in the desert He is prepared to deliver you.

What a gift! God's heart is for you to be free from burdens, free from the darkness, and free to proclaim with thanksgiving all that He has done in your life so that others might draw closer to Him. Your story of thanksgiving could be the very light someone in your life needs most this holiday season to move them toward the freedom and restoration God so willingly offers.

PRAYER

Father God, today, even in the middle of my mess, when I feel like I'm still wandering, I want to proclaim Your goodness, Your great gifts, and Your amazing love. Thank You for knowing me, loving me, and inviting me into Your perfect rest. Amen.

WEEK 2
Tuesday

READ

Philippians 4:10–20

I have great joy in the Lord because now at last you have again expressed your concern for me. (Now I know you were concerned before but had no opportunity to do anything.) 11 I am not saying this because I am in need, for I have learned to be content in any circumstance. 12 I have experienced times of need and times of abundance. In any and every circumstance I have learned the secret of contentment, whether I go satisfied or hungry, have plenty or nothing. 13 I am able to do all things through the one who strengthens me. 14 Nevertheless, you did well to share with me in my trouble. 15 And as you Philippians know, at the beginning of my gospel ministry, when I left Macedonia, no church shared with me in this matter of giving and receiving except you alone. 16 For even in Thessalonica on more than one occasion you sent something for my need. 17 I do not say this because I am seeking a gift. Rather, I seek the credit that abounds to your account. 18 For I have received everything, and I have plenty. I have all I need because I received from Epaphroditus what you sent—a fragrant offering, an acceptable sacrifice, very pleasing to God. 19 And my God will supply your every need according to his glorious riches in Christ Jesus. 20 May glory be given to God our Father forever and ever. Amen.

SOAP

WEEK 2 • TUESDAY

SOAP / *Philippians 4:18–19*
SCRIPTURE / *Write out the SOAP verses*

OBSERVATION / *Write 3 - 4 observations*

APPLICATION / *Write down 1 - 2 applications*

PRAYER / *Write out a prayer over what you learned*

DEVOTIONAL
WEEK 2 • TUESDAY

SOAP

Philippians 4:18–19

For I have received everything, and I have plenty. I have all I need because I received from Epaphroditus what you sent—a fragrant offering, an acceptable sacrifice, very pleasing to God. And my God will supply your every need according to his glorious riches in Christ Jesus.

INTO THE TEXT

In a world that screams at us that we need to buy more, have more, do more, Jesus gives us a beautiful counter-culture option to quiet the shouts: contentment. When I was little my Christmas wish list was made up of all the latest toys I saw during Saturday morning cartoons, or the cutest outfits I'd circled in the department store catalog that arrived in our mailbox in November. Add in social media and YouTube reviews and my daughter has an even longer—and more complicated—wish list of her own, full of items I know she neither needs nor will enjoy much longer than Christmas morning.

Maybe you have a similar process in your home, but as any gift-giving holiday approaches, we take a careful look at all the "things" we already have. We find some items that we are happy to share with a friend, or items that we know will bring someone else more joy so we can make room for something new. But ultimately, we take a long hard look at how grateful and content we've been with what we already have. Are the "must have" toys and games tossed in a corner, collecting dust or already broken? Have we taken care of what we already have in a way that shows that we're ready for what's next?

When Paul wrote this letter to the Philippians, he shared that he discovered the secret to a joy-filled life: finding contentment no matter his circumstances. Whether in times of need or times of abundance, whether he was living freely or in jail, whether he was hungry or satisfied, Paul was content because he found joy in the Lord. Paul knew he was weak and that Jesus would provide all that he needed. God will do the same for us. Let's give Him thanks!

PRAYER

God, You are generous and loving, and I am so grateful that—no matter my circumstances—You are always more than enough. Help me take some time to pause and reflect with a grateful heart on all that You have done in my life so I can be content and full of Your joy this season. Amen.

WEEK 2
Wednesday

READ

Luke 6:37–38

Do not judge, and you will not be judged; do not condemn, and you will not be condemned; forgive, and you will be forgiven. 38 Give, and it will be given to you: A good measure, pressed down, shaken together, running over, will be poured into your lap. For the measure you use will be the measure you receive.

2 Corinthians 9

For it is not necessary for me to write you about this service to the saints, 2 because I know your eagerness to help. I keep boasting to the Macedonians about this eagerness of yours, that Achaia has been ready to give since last year, and your zeal to participate has stirred up most of them. 3 But I am sending these brothers so that our boasting about you may not be empty in this case, so that you may be ready just as I kept telling them. 4 For if any of the Macedonians should come with me and find that you are not ready to give, we would be humiliated (not to mention you) by this confidence we had in you. 5 Therefore I thought it necessary to urge these brothers to go to you in advance and to arrange ahead of time the generous contribution you had promised, so this may be ready as a generous gift and not as something you feel forced to do. 6 My point is this: The person who sows sparingly will also reap sparingly, and the person who sows generously will also reap generously. 7 Each one of you should give just as he has decided in his heart, not reluctantly or under compulsion, because God loves a cheerful giver. 8 And God is able to make all grace overflow to you so that because you have enough of everything in every way at all times, you will overflow in every good work. 9 Just as it is written, "***He has scattered widely, he has given to the poor; his righteousness remains forever.***" 10 Now God who provides seed for the sower and bread for food will provide and multiply your supply of seed and will cause the harvest of your righteousness to grow. 11 You will be enriched in every way so that you may be generous on every occasion, which is producing through us thanksgiving to God, 12 because the service of this ministry is not only providing for the needs of the saints but is also overflowing with many thanks to God. 13 Through the evidence of this service they will glorify God because of your obedience to your confession in the gospel of Christ and the generosity of your sharing with them and with everyone. 14 And in their prayers on your behalf, they long for you because of the extraordinary grace God has shown to you. 15 Thanks be to God for his indescribable gift!

SOAP

WEEK 2 • WEDNESDAY

SOAP / *2 Corinthians 9:7–8*
SCRIPTURE / *Write out the SOAP verses*

OBSERVATION / *Write 3 - 4 observations*

APPLICATION / *Write down 1 - 2 applications*

PRAYER / *Write out a prayer over what you learned*

DEVOTIONAL
WEEK 2 • WEDNESDAY

SOAP

2 Corinthians 9:7–8

Each one of you should give just as he has decided in his heart, not reluctantly or under compulsion, because God loves a cheerful giver. And God is able to make all grace overflow to you so that because you have enough of everything in every way at all times, you will overflow in every good work.

INTO THE TEXT

Have you ever been forced to participate in a gift exchange, maybe at work or with a group you aren't particularly close with? Buying a present for your loved ones is fun and easy. You know them and you want them to be happy with their gifts. Giving out of obligation is a challenge, not only by adding the dreaded "one more thing" to our overwhelmed schedules, but to our creativity, our attitudes, and our resources.

It's how we end up with a random assortment of candles, dish towels, and interesting garden decorations that we'll never display.

There is something special about receiving a gift we know was chosen with love. We open it with excitement and we cherish the gift even when it might not be what we expected. God wants us to be cheerful in our giving, not helping others out of a sense of obligation, guilt, or coercion, but from a place of love.

When we love God and love others, it's a blessing to be able to meet the needs of those around us. It's a joy to serve, to give of our time and share our skills with others, not because of what we can get in return but because it puts to good use the gifts God has so generously given us. It shows others that we care about and honor them more than our comfort.

Giving isn't always easy. But we can trust that God can do more with the gifts we give than we could ever imagine.

PRAYER

Father, I know You love a cheerful giver. May my eyes be open and my heart alert for ways to serve others in this season, willing and able to give generously and with love as I honor others. Thank You for showing me what it means to give everything through the life of Your Son, Jesus. Amen.

WEEK 2
Thursday

READ

Ephesians 5:15–20

Therefore consider carefully how you live—not as unwise but as wise, 16 taking advantage of every opportunity, because the days are evil. 17 For this reason do not be foolish, but be wise by understanding what the Lord's will is. 18 And do not get drunk with wine, which is debauchery, but be filled by the Spirit, 19 speaking to one another in psalms, hymns, and spiritual songs, singing and making music in your hearts to the Lord, 20 always giving thanks to God the Father for all things in the name of our Lord Jesus Christ

1 Thessalonians 5:16–18

Always rejoice, 17 constantly pray, 18 in everything give thanks. For this is God's will for you in Christ Jesus.

SOAP

WEEK 2 • THURSDAY

SOAP / *1 Thessalonians 5:16–18*
SCRIPTURE / *Write out the SOAP verses*

OBSERVATION / *Write 3 - 4 observations*

APPLICATION / *Write down 1 - 2 applications*

PRAYER / *Write out a prayer over what you learned*

DEVOTIONAL
WEEK 2 • THURSDAY

SOAP

1 Thessalonians 5:16–18

Always rejoice, constantly pray, in everything give thanks. For this is God's will for you in Christ Jesus.

INTO THE TEXT

As our calendars fill with good things and our to-do lists become longer, it can be easy to switch into auto-pilot. We have places to be, things to do, people to see, and suddenly the joy of this season fades away, replaced by obligations instead of celebration. Our amazing Father knew we would find ourselves in these situations and has given us a way to move through it:

Give thanks.

Scripture instructs us to give thanks, not only at meals or before we fall asleep at night, but in all circumstances. Grumbling and gratitude cannot coexist, so if you are feeling overwhelmed, busy, unsure, or discouraged, unwrap the gift of gratitude God has given you and speak it over your circumstances.

Even when things are hard, plans don't go the way you expected, you have to say "no" to something good to leave room for something great, or expectations are unmet, look for what you can thank God for in that situation.

Living a life full of gratitude, especially when it's not easy, will be a light in the darkness to those around you. Your example will be a gift to show that your love for God is more important than your love for your plans. It might just be the one thing someone else needs to experience to love God greatly.

PRAYER

God, You love me so much that You have even prepared a way for my heart and mind to stay focused on You in all circumstances. As this season becomes busy and my attention is pulled in a million little directions, help me to swap grumbling for gratitude so I can be a light to those around me. In all circumstances, I give thanks to You, because even when things don't go my way, I trust and believe that Your way is better. Amen.

WEEK 2
Friday

READ

Psalm 100
A thanksgiving psalm.

Shout out praises to the LORD, all the earth! 2 Worship the LORD with joy. Enter his presence with joyful singing. 3 Acknowledge that the LORD is God. He made us and we belong to him, we are his people, the sheep of his pasture. 4 Enter his gates with thanksgiving, and his courts with praise. Give him thanks. Praise his name. 5 For the LORD is good. His loyal love endures, and he is faithful through all generations.

SOAP

WEEK 2 • FRIDAY

SOAP / *Psalm 100:1–5*
SCRIPTURE / *Write out the SOAP verses*

OBSERVATION / *Write 3 - 4 observations*

APPLICATION / *Write down 1 - 2 applications*

PRAYER / *Write out a prayer over what you learned*

DEVOTIONAL
WEEK 2 • FRIDAY

SOAP

Psalm 100:1-5

Shout out praises to the Lord, all the earth! Worship the Lord with joy. Enter his presence with joyful singing. Acknowledge that the Lord is God. He made us and we belong to him, we are his people, the sheep of his pasture. Enter his gates with thanksgiving, and his courts with praise. Give him thanks. Praise his name. For the Lord is good. His loyal love endures, and he is faithful through all generations.

INTO THE TEXT

Have you ever heard a hymn, worship song, or Christmas carol that made you feel more deeply connected to God? Maybe it revealed a part of His character that You never knew about, or the lyrics spoke hope and healing over the situation you were facing. Music is a gift that helps us tell stories, sing praises, and celebrate who God is, what He has done, and what He will do.

The writer of today's psalm was celebrating Israel's special relationship to God and invited everyone to praise God for His faithfulness. This wasn't a "stand and mumble your way through the words" kind of corporate worship—no, this came with a special instruction to worship with joy!

Let's take a note from the psalmist's example and write out our own psalm of praise today. What is it about God that you want to acknowledge and praise with a joyful heart? What gifts has God given you that you can thank Him for? Where have you experienced God's love and faithfulness in your life this year? What prayers has He answered? What does it mean to you that God made you, called you to be part of His forever family, and watches over you?

Pray or sing your words back to God with as much joy as your heart can hold! Our God is good and worthy of our praise!

If you don't know what to praise God for today, why not start by praying today's Scripture back to Him?

PRAYER

Lord, You alone are God. You made me and claimed me as Yours. You invited me into Your family and You protect and provide for me! God, You are good and I thank You for Your enduring love and faithfulness. Amen.

REFLECT
WEEK 2

1. How can you proclaim what God has done in your life? Think of ways to make proclaiming God's goodness a daily habit.

   ....
   ....
   ....

2. How has God supplied your every need in the past? Do you believe He is both willing and able to meet all your needs in the future?

   ....
   ....
   ....

3. What does it mean to be a cheerful giver? How can you give cheerfully and willingly today?

   ....
   ....
   ....

4. What is God's will for you, according to 1 Thessalonians 5:16–18?

   ....
   ....
   ....

5. How have you seen God's goodness in your life this week? Praise Him for His goodness today!

   ....
   ....
   ....

JOURNAL
your thoughts

JOURNAL
your thoughts

WEEK 3

*Not only this,
but we also rejoice
in sufferings,
knowing that
suffering produces
endurance, and
endurance, character,
and character,
hope. And hope
does not disappoint,
because the love
of God has been
poured out in our
hearts through the
Holy Spirit who
was given to us.*

Romans 5:3–5

PRAY

Write down your prayer requests and praises for this week.

....
....
....
....
....
....
....
....
....
....
....
....

WEEKLY CHALLENGE

In Romans 5:3–5, Paul tells us our hope in Christ does not disappoint us. Have you found this to be true? Have you ever felt disappointed by hope? How can you be certain that your hope in Christ will never disappoint?

....
....
....
....
....
....
....

WEEK 3
Monday

READ

Romans 5:1–11

Therefore, since we have been declared righteous by faith, we have peace with God through our Lord Jesus Christ, 2 through whom we have also obtained access into this grace in which we stand, and we rejoice in the hope of God's glory. 3 Not only this, but we also rejoice in sufferings, knowing that suffering produces endurance, 4 and endurance, character, and character, hope. 5 And hope does not disappoint, because the love of God has been poured out in our hearts through the Holy Spirit who was given to us. 6 For while we were still helpless, at the right time Christ died for the ungodly. 7 (For rarely will anyone die for a righteous person, though for a good person perhaps someone might possibly dare to die.) 8 But God demonstrates his own love for us, in that while we were still sinners, Christ died for us. 9 Much more then, because we have now been declared righteous by his blood, we will be saved through him from God's wrath.10 For if while we were enemies we were reconciled to God through the death of his Son, how much more, since we have been reconciled, will we be saved by his life? 11 Not only this, but we also rejoice in God through our Lord Jesus Christ, through whom we have now received this reconciliation.

SOAP

WEEK 3 · MONDAY

SOAP / *Romans 5:3–5*
SCRIPTURE / *Write out the SOAP verses*

OBSERVATION / *Write 3 - 4 observations*

APPLICATION / *Write down 1 - 2 applications*

PRAYER / *Write out a prayer over what you learned*

DEVOTIONAL
WEEK 3 • MONDAY

SOAP

Romans 5:3–5

Not only this, but we also rejoice in sufferings, knowing that suffering produces endurance, and endurance, character, and character, hope. And hope does not disappoint, because the love of God has been poured out in our hearts through the Holy Spirit who was given to us.

INTO THE TEXT

This week of Advent we will spend time focused on God's gift of hope, and what a beautiful gift it is! The hope we have is not dependent on our circumstances, success, what we own, or what we can accomplish. Our hope has nothing to do with the titles we hold, the work we do, how often we volunteer, or how well-behaved our kids are. Our hope is in God—and it's a hope that never changes or disappoints!

Unlike the world's version of hope that expects everything to be easy, our hope is strongest when it comes from the development of our character through challenges. When we know that the end result of our suffering is hope and a life that is more like Christ, we can face anything that comes our way with our eyes focused on God and our heads held high.

It is through suffering that endurance is produced, which gives us what we need to press on in our faith as we learn to rest, not stop. As we develop our endurance our character is refined, separating us from those who would give up or give in when times are hard. We embrace the counter-cultural lifestyle of God's kingdom that says that, when we are weak, God is strong. We invite others into our lives to help us run this race well, and we cheer for and love those the world would consider our competition.

And in the end, after endurance and character, our suffering produces hope. Hope that isn't about us, but is an overflow of the love that God has poured into our hearts. When our worlds are shaken, this hope stands firm, because God's love never changes.

PRAYER

God, You are my hope. When life is hard, help me focus on the gifts You have for me as my character is refined to be more like Christ. The hope I have in You is unshakable because Your love for me is unchanging. Amen.

WEEK 3

Tuesday

READ

Hebrews 10:19–25

Therefore, brothers and sisters, since we have confidence to enter the sanctuary by the blood of Jesus, 20 by the fresh and living way that he inaugurated for us through the curtain, that is, through his flesh, 21 and since we have a great priest over the house of God, 22 let us draw near with a sincere heart in the assurance that faith brings, because we have had our hearts sprinkled clean from an evil conscience and our bodies washed in pure water. 23 And let us hold unwaveringly to the hope that we confess, for the one who made the promise is trustworthy. 24 And let us take thought of how to spur one another on to love and good works, 25 not abandoning our own meetings, as some are in the habit of doing, but encouraging each other, and even more so because you see the day drawing near.

SOAP

WEEK 3 • TUESDAY

SOAP / *Hebrews 10:23*
SCRIPTURE / *Write out the SOAP verses*

OBSERVATION / *Write 3 - 4 observations*

APPLICATION / *Write down 1 - 2 applications*

PRAYER / *Write out a prayer over what you learned*

DEVOTIONAL
WEEK 3 • TUESDAY

SOAP

Hebrews 10:23

And let us hold unwaveringly to the hope that we confess, for the one who made the promise is trustworthy.

INTO THE TEXT

Throughout the Bible, God makes and keeps promises to His children. He promised Abram that he would be the father of many nations (Genesis 17:4); God promised to protect the people of Israel and free them from 430 years of slavery (Exodus 2:24–25); and God promised salvation to all who believe in His Son (Romans 1:16–17).

God also promises that:
If we seek Him, we will find Him (Deuteronomy 4:29).
His love will never fail (1 Chronicles 16:34).
We will receive new life in Christ (2 Corinthians 5:17).
We will find peace when we pray (Philippians 4:6–7).
He will supply our needs (Matthew 6:33).
...and so much more!

The gift of hope that God gives us is a solid foundation for our faith, because the promises God made to the men and women in the Bible show us His incredible promise-keeping character. When we take the time to search God's Word for proof of His character, we will find more examples than we would ever be able to share. But the most powerful example of God's trustworthiness to your friends, family, and community is the way you live out the hope you have in Him.

God has kept His promises to you, too. Have you shared that with anyone lately? Have you told someone about the peace, love, and comforting presence of God you've experienced when you needed Him most?

I can't help but think of the old hymn that says, "My hope is built on nothing less than Jesus' blood and righteousness." God promised us a Redeemer, and kept that promise through the birth, death, and resurrection of His Son.

PRAYER

Father, thank You for including me in the promises You've made to Your children. My hope comes from You. Help me share the source of my hope with those around me as we celebrate Your Son. Amen.

WEEK 3
Wednesday

READ

Romans 15:7–13

Receive one another, then, just as Christ also received you, to God's glory. 8 For I tell you that Christ has become a servant of the circumcised on behalf of God's truth to confirm the promises made to the fathers, 9 and thus the Gentiles glorify God for his mercy. As it is written, "*Because of this I will confess you among the Gentiles, and I will sing praises to your name.*" 10 And again it says: "*Rejoice, O Gentiles, with his people.*" 11 And again, "*Praise the Lord all you Gentiles, and let all the peoples praise him.*" 12 And again Isaiah says, "*The root of Jesse will come, and the one who rises to rule over the Gentiles, in him will the Gentiles hope.*" 13 Now may the God of hope fill you with all joy and peace as you believe in him, so that you may abound in hope by the power of the Holy Spirit.

SOAP

WEEK 3 • WEDNESDAY

SOAP / *Romans 15:13*
SCRIPTURE / *Write out the SOAP verses*

OBSERVATION / *Write 3 - 4 observations*

APPLICATION / *Write down 1 - 2 applications*

PRAYER / *Write out a prayer over what you learned*

DEVOTIONAL
WEEK 3 • WEDNESDAY

SOAP

Romans 15:13

Now may the God of hope fill you with all joy and peace as you believe in him, so that you may abound in hope by the power of the Holy Spirit.

INTO THE TEXT

Our God, the great Giver, has given us an amazing Gift in His Son, Jesus. Unlike the gifts we receive from friends or family, this is a gift that keeps giving, because when we accept God's free gift of salvation through Jesus, we continue to receive good gifts!

Gifts always require some kind of sacrifice, and in Paul's letter to the Roman believers he reminded them that Jesus has given us the perfect example to follow. Jesus put aside everything He could have easily claimed—all His rights and privileges as the Son of God—and instead sacrificed His life so that we could receive the gift of salvation. Instead of finding ways to be divisive, Paul encouraged the believers (including us) to follow Jesus' example, loving others well, working together, and embracing the gift of hope and power that we receive from the Holy Spirit.

God did not send His Son to be born as a human and die for our sins and then leave us to figure the rest out on our own. God is good, it is His nature, and the hope that He desires for us comes from an overflow of what we receive from Him, through the Holy Spirit. This is a hope that does not fade. This is a hope that shines brightly when everything around us feels dark.

When we place our hope in Christ and rely on the help and power of the Holy Spirit, nothing can take it away. The Jesus we celebrate at Christmas was a promise God kept to His people—a promise of salvation and freedom from sin and the things that keep us from living abundant, full lives for His glory. That is a gift that keeps giving!

PRAYER

Father God, thank You for sending Your only Son to be born so I would have a way back to You. This Christmas, help me remember to keep my heart focused on You, the solid foundation of my hope. Amen.

WEEK 3

Thursday

READ

Romans 8:18–25

For I consider that our present sufferings cannot even be compared to the coming glory that will be revealed to us. 19 For the creation eagerly waits for the revelation of the sons of God. 20 For the creation was subjected to futility—not willingly but because of God who subjected it—in hope 21 that the creation itself will also be set free from the bondage of decay into the glorious freedom of God's children. 22 For we know that the whole creation groans and suffers together until now. 23 Not only this, but we ourselves also, who have the firstfruits of the Spirit, groan inwardly as we eagerly await our adoption, the redemption of our bodies. 24 For in hope we were saved. Now hope that is seen is not hope, because who hopes for what he sees? 25 But if we hope for what we do not see, we eagerly wait for it with endurance.

SOAP

WEEK 3 • THURSDAY

SOAP / *Romans 8:24–25*
SCRIPTURE / *Write out the SOAP verses*

OBSERVATION / *Write 3 - 4 observations*

APPLICATION / *Write down 1 - 2 applications*

PRAYER / *Write out a prayer over what you learned*

DEVOTIONAL
WEEK 3 • THURSDAY

SOAP

Romans 8:24–25

For in hope we were saved. Now hope that is seen is not hope, because who hopes for what he sees? But if we hope for what we do not see, we eagerly wait for it with endurance.

INTO THE TEXT

What kind of gift recipient are you? Do you like to take your time as you open the gift, carefully unwrapping each layer of ribbon and paper, enjoying the process and anticipation as much as the outcome? Are you a gift shaker, someone who likes to poke, press, tumble, and twist their present with eyes closed to try to guess what is inside before opening it because you love the thrill of a correct guess just as much as the present? Or maybe you just rip right in, tossing paper and bows to the side with wild abandon because you just can't wait a second longer to see what's inside?

Now take that feeling of excitement and apply it to the holy anticipation of the coming reality of Christ's long-awaited return, the final piece of our promised salvation when all is made new.

In Paul's letter to the Romans he reminded them to keep their hope on the kingdom God has promised, not what they saw around them. The eagerness we feel when receiving a gift at Christmas loses some of its spark when we're handed a gift with no wrapping. We see it. We know what it is. We miss out on the opportunity to hope for something special because we're immediately faced with reality.

Paul tells us to keep our hope fixed on what we can't see—the perfect work of salvation that God is doing on our behalf—and to continue to wait on what God has promised with endurance or perseverance. As we unwrap gifts this Christmas, may each moment of hope in the unknown remind us to press forward with hope in what God still has yet to do in our lives, for His kingdom.

PRAYER

God, thank You that we can take moments of this special season, when we celebrate Your Son, to grow closer to You. Help our faith and hope increase as we connect our feelings of excitement and anticipation with the eagerness we feel about the return of Jesus, our Savior. Amen.

WEEK 3
Friday

READ

Psalm 105

Give thanks to the Lord. Call on his name. Make known his accomplishments among the nations. 2 Sing to him. Make music to him. Tell about all his miraculous deeds. 3 Boast about his holy name. Let the hearts of those who seek the Lord rejoice. 4 Seek the Lord and the strength he gives. Seek his presence continually. 5 Recall the miraculous deeds he performed, his mighty acts and the judgments he decreed, 6 O children of Abraham, God's servant, you descendants of Jacob, God's chosen ones. 7 He is the Lord our God; he carries out judgment throughout the earth. 8 He always remembers his covenantal decree, the promise he made to a thousand generations— 9 the promise he made to Abraham, the promise he made by oath to Isaac. 10 He gave it to Jacob as a decree, to Israel as a lasting promise, 11 saying, "To you I will give the land of Canaan as the portion of your inheritance." 12 When they were few in number, just a very few, and resident foreigners within it, 13 they wandered from nation to nation, and from one kingdom to another. 14 He let no one oppress them; he disciplined kings for their sake, 15 saying, "Don't touch my chosen ones. Don't harm my prophets." 16 He called down a famine upon the earth; he cut off all the food supply. 17 He sent a man ahead of them— Joseph was sold as a servant. 18 The shackles hurt his feet; his neck was placed in an iron collar, 19 until the time when his prediction came true. The Lord's word proved him right. 20 The king authorized his release; the ruler of nations set him free. 21 He put him in charge of his palace, and made him manager of all his property, 22 giving him authority to imprison his officials and to teach his advisers. 23 Israel moved to Egypt; Jacob lived for a time in the land of Ham. 24 The Lord made his people very fruitful, and made

WEEK 3
Friday

Psalm 105 (continued)

them more numerous than their enemies. 25 He caused the Egyptians to hate his people, and to mistreat his servants. 26 He sent his servant Moses, and Aaron, whom he had chosen. 27 They executed his miraculous signs among them, and his amazing deeds in the land of Ham. 28 He made it dark; Moses and Aaron did not disobey his orders. 29 He turned the Egyptians' water into blood, and killed their fish. 30 Their land was overrun by frogs, which even got into the rooms of their kings. 31 He ordered flies to come; gnats invaded their whole territory. 32 He sent hail along with the rain; there was lightning in their land. 33 He destroyed their vines and fig trees, and broke the trees throughout their territory. 34 He ordered locusts to come, innumerable grasshoppers. 35 They ate all the vegetation in their land, and devoured the crops of their fields. 36 He struck down all the firstborn in their land, the firstfruits of their reproductive power. 37 He brought his people out enriched with silver and gold; none of his tribes stumbled. 38 Egypt was happy when they left, for they were afraid of them. 39 He spread out a cloud for a cover, and provided a fire to light up the night. 40 They asked for food, and he sent quail; he satisfied them with food from the sky. 41 He opened up a rock and water flowed out; a river ran through dry regions. 42 Yes, he remembered the sacred promise he made to Abraham his servant. 43 When he led his people out, they rejoiced; his chosen ones shouted with joy. 44 He handed the territory of nations over to them, and they took possession of what other peoples had produced, 45 so that they might keep his commands and obey his laws. Praise the Lord.

"In the creation, God gave us ourselves; in the redemption, He gave us Himself."

Thomas Watson

SOAP

WEEK 3 · FRIDAY

SOAP / *Psalm 105:42–43*
SCRIPTURE / *Write out the SOAP verses*

OBSERVATION / *Write 3 - 4 observations*

APPLICATION / *Write down 1 - 2 applications*

PRAYER / *Write out a prayer over what you learned*

DEVOTIONAL
WEEK 3 • FRIDAY

SOAP

Psalm 105:42–43

Yes, he remembered the sacred promise he made to Abraham his servant. When he led his people out, they rejoiced; his chosen ones shouted with joy.

INTO THE TEXT

The Psalmist of today's Scripture begins by inviting all people to take ownership of their relationship with and worship of God. We're to: give thanks, call on, make known, sing, make music, tell about, boast, rejoice, seek, and recall.

We then read a recap of the history of the Israelites, from God's first promise to Abraham to the fulfillment of that promise as the people entered Canaan. In His perfect timing, God kept His word to His people, and through their worship and praise they could tell the story of His faithfulness.

What is your story of God's faithfulness? Where has He kept His promises, filled you with hope, delivered you from sin, walked with you through the wilderness, provided what you needed most? Give thanks to God today! Call on His name and make known what He has done in your life to all nations—to your family, neighbors, and community. Sing back to God what He has done in your life, or play music that helps to share your story.

Go ahead and boast about what God has done in your life and give your heart permission to rejoice! The Israelites weren't perfect, and neither are we. But our God is, and He remains faithful to His children. Don't allow the shame of past mistakes to keep you from receiving the gift of praising God. What He has done for us, through Jesus, covers it all.

PRAYER

God, today we praise You for Your faithfulness. You kept Your promise and sent us a Redeemer so that our stories would not end with the wandering, but with our wonderful reunion with You. Help us to tell the story You are writing in our lives so that others might hear and believe in You, too. Amen.

REFLECT

WEEK 3

1. How does suffering produce endurance? Have you experienced this in your life?

   ....
   ....
   ....

2. How do you know that Christ is trustworthy? How does His trustworthy character give you confidence as you hope in Him?

   ....
   ....
   ....

3. What does it mean to abound in hope?

   ....
   ....
   ....

4. How are hope and endurance connected? Can you have hope without endurance? Can you endure without hope?

   ....
   ....
   ....

5. God always keeps His promises, and you can place your hope in Him. How can you give thanks for the gift of hope today?

   ....
   ....
   ....

JOURNAL
your thoughts

JOURNAL
your thoughts

WEEK 4

Now (faith) is being <u>sure</u> of what we hope for, being <u>convinced</u> of what we do not see.

Hebrews 11:1

PRAY

Write down your prayer requests and praises for this week.

....
....
....
....
....
....
....
....
....
....
....
....
....

WEEKLY CHALLENGE

This week, take time to meditate on the gift of faith. How is faith a gift? In what ways has your faith been a gift in your life? How can you be sure of your faith when you cannot see the object of your faith?

....
....
....
....
....
....
....

WEEK 4
Monday

READ

Hebrews 11

Now faith is being sure of what we hope for, being convinced of what we do not see. 2 For by it the people of old received God's commendation. 3 By faith we understand that the worlds were set in order at God's command, so that the visible has its origin in the invisible. 4 By faith Abel offered God a greater sacrifice than Cain, and through his faith he was commended as righteous, because God commended him for his offerings. And through his faith he still speaks, though he is dead. 5 By faith Enoch was taken up so that he did not see death, and he was not to be found because God took him up. For before his removal he had been commended as having pleased God. 6 Now without faith it is impossible to please him, for the one who approaches God must believe that he exists and that he rewards those who seek him. 7 By faith Noah, when he was warned about things not yet seen, with reverent regard constructed an ark for the deliverance of his family. Through faith he condemned the world and became an heir of the righteousness that comes by faith. 8 By faith Abraham obeyed when he was called to go out to a place he would later receive as an inheritance, and he went out without understanding where he was going. 9 By faith he lived as a foreigner in the promised land as though it were a foreign country, living in tents with Isaac and Jacob, who were fellow heirs of the same promise. 10 For he was looking forward to the city with firm foundations, whose architect and builder is God. 11 By faith, even though Sarah herself was barren and he was too old, he received the ability to procreate, because he regarded the one who had given the promise to be trustworthy. 12 So in fact children were fathered by one

WEEK 4
Monday

Hebrews 11 (continued)

man—and this one as good as dead—*like the number of stars in the sky and like the innumerable grains of sand on the seashore.* 13 These all died in faith without receiving the things promised, but they saw them in the distance and welcomed them and acknowledged that they were strangers and foreigners on the earth. 14 For those who speak in such a way make it clear that they are seeking a homeland. 15 In fact, if they had been thinking of the land that they had left, they would have had opportunity to return. 16 But as it is, they aspire to a better land, that is, a heavenly one. Therefore, God is not ashamed to be called their God, for he has prepared a city for them. 17 By faith Abraham, when he was tested, offered up Isaac. He had received the promises, yet he was ready to offer up his only son. 18 God had told him, "**Through Isaac descendants will carry on your name**," 19 and he reasoned that God could even raise him from the dead, and in a sense he received him back from there. 20 By faith also Isaac blessed Jacob and Esau concerning the future. 21 By faith Jacob, as he was dying, blessed each of the sons of Joseph and **worshiped as he leaned on his staff**. 22 By faith Joseph, at the end of his life, mentioned the exodus of the sons of Israel and gave instructions about his burial. 23 By faith, when Moses was born, his parents hid him for three months, because they saw the child was beautiful and they were not afraid of the king's edict. 24 By faith, when he grew up, Moses refused to be called the son of Pharaoh's daughter, 25 choosing rather to be ill-treated with the people of God than to enjoy sin's fleeting pleasure. 26 He regarded abuse suffered for Christ to be greater wealth than the treasures of Egypt, for his eyes were fixed on the reward. 27 By faith he left Egypt without fearing the king's anger, for he persevered as though he could see the one who is invisible. 28 By faith

WEEK 4
Monday

Hebrews 11 (continued)

he kept the Passover and the sprinkling of the blood, so that the one who destroyed the firstborn would not touch them. 29 By faith they crossed the Red Sea as if on dry ground, but when the Egyptians tried it, they were swallowed up. 30 By faith the walls of Jericho fell after the people marched around them for seven days. 31 By faith Rahab the prostitute escaped the destruction of the disobedient, because she welcomed the spies in peace. 32 And what more shall I say? For time will fail me if I tell of Gideon, Barak, Samson, Jephthah, of David and Samuel and the prophets. 33 Through faith they conquered kingdoms, administered justice, gained what was promised, shut the mouths of lions, 34 quenched raging fire, escaped the edge of the sword, gained strength in weakness, became mighty in battle, put foreign armies to flight, 35 and women received back their dead raised to life. But others were tortured, not accepting release, to obtain resurrection to a better life. 36 And others experienced mocking and flogging, and even chains and imprisonment. 37 They were stoned, sawed apart, murdered with the sword; they went about in sheepskins and goatskins; they were destitute, afflicted, ill-treated 38 (the world was not worthy of them); they wandered in deserts and mountains and caves and openings in the earth. 39 And these all were commended for their faith, yet they did not receive what was promised. 40 For God had provided something better for us, so that they would be made perfect together with us.

SOAP

WEEK 4 · MONDAY

SOAP / *Hebrews 11:1, 6*
SCRIPTURE / *Write out the SOAP verses*

OBSERVATION / *Write 3 - 4 observations*

APPLICATION / *Write down 1 - 2 applications*

PRAYER / *Write out a prayer over what you learned*

DEVOTIONAL
WEEK 4 • MONDAY

SOAP

Hebrews 11:1, 6

Now faith is being sure of what we hope for, being convinced of what we do not see.

Now without faith it is impossible to please him, for the one who approaches God must believe that he exists and that he rewards those who seek him.

INTO THE TEXT

The dictionary defines faith as "confidence or trust in a person or thing; a belief that is not based on proof." The Bible defines faith as "being sure of what we hope for, being convinced of what we do not see" (Hebrews 11:1).

The gift of faith God has given us is different from the version the world understands, because while we might have hope in what we have not seen, we do have proof! God's Word is our proof that God loves us, has a good plan for us, and has a place for us in His family. Hebrews 11 is a great place to begin, as the author gives us example after example of men and women who showed great faith in God and the outcome of their faith.

By faith, Abel offered God a great sacrifice, and by faith God commended him as righteous. Enoch's faith pleased God, and as a result, Enoch did not face a natural death. By faith, Noah built the ark God designed, and by faith God delivered Noah's family. Abraham and Sarah's faith stood the test of time, and although they did not see all of God's promises happen in their lifetime, their faith was rewarded for many generations.

When our faith is placed in people or circumstances, the outcome will usually be disappointment. When our faith is placed in God, He will never let us down. In fact, our reading today says that God rewards those who seek Him and believe in Him. Only faith in God results in a continued pouring out of gifts, beyond what we could ask for or imagine, and sometimes beyond what we will live to experience. Our faith in God will leave a legacy that will impact generations!

PRAYER

Heavenly Father, it is amazing that You would design this relationship in such a beautiful way, that my faith in You becomes a blessing. Thank You for the examples of the men and women in Your Word that encourage me to continue believing and hoping in what I can't yet see. Amen.

WEEK 4
Tuesday

READ

Matthew 17:14–20

When they came to the crowd, a man came to him, knelt before him, 15 and said, "Lord, have mercy on my son, because he has seizures and suffers terribly, for he often falls into the fire and into the water. 16 I brought him to your disciples, but they were not able to heal him." 17 Jesus answered, "You unbelieving and perverse generation! How much longer must I be with you? How much longer must I endure you? Bring him here to me." 18 Then Jesus rebuked the demon and it came out of him, and the boy was healed from that moment. 19 Then the disciples came to Jesus privately and said, "Why couldn't we cast it out?" 20 He told them, "It was because of your little faith. I tell you the truth, if you have faith the size of a mustard seed, you will say to this mountain, 'Move from here to there,' and it will move; nothing will be impossible for you."

Matthew 21:18–22

Now early in the morning, as he returned to the city, he was hungry. 19 After noticing a fig tree by the road he went to it, but found nothing on it except leaves. He said to it, "Never again will there be fruit from you!" And the fig tree withered at once. 20 When the disciples saw it they were amazed, saying, "How did the fig tree wither so quickly?" 21 Jesus answered them, "I tell you the truth, if you have faith and do not doubt, not only will you do what was done to the fig tree, but even if you say to this mountain, 'Be lifted up and thrown into the sea,' it will happen. 22 And whatever you ask in prayer, if you believe, you will receive."

SOAP

WEEK 4 • TUESDAY

SOAP / *Matthew 21:21–22*
SCRIPTURE / *Write out the SOAP verses*

OBSERVATION / *Write 3 - 4 observations*

APPLICATION / *Write down 1 - 2 applications*

PRAYER / *Write out a prayer over what you learned*

DEVOTIONAL
WEEK 4 • TUESDAY

SOAP

Matthew 21:21–22

Jesus answered them, "I tell you the truth, if you have faith and do not doubt, not only will you do what was done to the fig tree, but even if you say to this mountain, 'Be lifted up and thrown into the sea,' it will happen. And whatever you ask in prayer, if you believe, you will receive."

INTO THE TEXT

Faith is a gift, and we don't need to have much of it for God to do something amazing with it. Matthew shared a moment with Jesus where He told Matthew that all it takes is faith the size of a mustard seed to move mountains. Have you ever seen a mustard seed? We have a jar of poppy seeds in our pantry that we use for baking, and a mustard seed is half the size of one of those!

Mustard plants, when given the right care, are hardy bushes that grow slowly, but can withstand high heat and little water. When fully grown, these plants are anywhere from six to twenty feet tall and have deep roots that seek out water, which helps them survive during droughts.

Our faith doesn't need to be big to have a big impact, but with proper nurturing and development, a commitment to slow but steady growth, and a willingness to dig our roots deep into God's Word and the Living Water of Jesus Christ, a tiny grain of faith can mature into something that can withstand our wilderness seasons.

Spend some time today reflecting on your faith. Ask God to reveal where you've been doubting or where you've been waiting to go to Him in prayer because your faith didn't feel big enough. Embrace your faith, whether it's as small as a mustard seed or feels twenty feet tall, and thank God for this beautiful gift that you can bring back to Him.

PRAYER

God, You promise that when I ask in faith and believe, I will receive—and that is a beautiful gift. Thank You for giving me all I need to nurture my mustard seed-sized faith into something amazing that You can use to move mountains. Amen.

WEEK 4
Wednesday

READ

Matthew 15:21–28

After going out from there, Jesus went to the region of Tyre and Sidon. 22 A Canaanite woman from that area came and cried out, "Have mercy on me, Lord, Son of David! My daughter is horribly demon-possessed!" 23 But he did not answer her a word. Then his disciples came and begged him, "Send her away, because she keeps on crying out after us." 24 So he answered, "I was sent only to the lost sheep of the house of Israel." 25 But she came and bowed down before him and said, "Lord, help me!" 26 "It is not right to take the children's bread and throw it to the dogs," he said. 27 "Yes, Lord," she replied, "but even the dogs eat the crumbs that fall from their masters' table." 28 Then Jesus answered her, "Woman, your faith is great! Let what you want be done for you." And her daughter was healed from that hour.

Luke 8:42–48

As Jesus was on his way, the crowds pressed around him. 43 Now a woman was there who had been suffering from a hemorrhage for twelve years but could not be healed by anyone. 44 She came up behind Jesus and touched the edge of his cloak, and at once the bleeding stopped. 45 Then Jesus asked, "Who was it who touched me?" When they all denied it, Peter said, "Master, the crowds are surrounding you and pressing against you!" 46 But Jesus said, "Someone touched me, for I know that power has gone out from me." 47 When the woman saw that she could not escape notice, she came trembling and fell down before him. In the presence of all the people, she explained why she had touched him and how she had been immediately healed. 48 Then he said to her, "Daughter, your faith has made you well. Go in peace."

SOAP
WEEK 4 • WEDNESDAY

SOAP / *Matthew 15:28; Luke 8:48*
SCRIPTURE / *Write out the SOAP verses*

OBSERVATION / *Write 3 - 4 observations*

APPLICATION / *Write down 1 - 2 applications*

PRAYER / *Write out a prayer over what you learned*

DEVOTIONAL
WEEK 4 • WEDNESDAY

SOAP

Matthew 15:28; Luke 8:48

Then Jesus answered her, "Woman, your faith is great! Let what you want be done for you." And her daughter was healed from that hour. Then he said to her, "Daughter, your faith has made you well. Go in peace."

INTO THE TEXT

The more we learn about God and the gifts He has given us, the more it feels like we're unwrapping a beautiful matryoshka doll. If you have ever played with one, you know these Russian nesting dolls open to reveal another doll, and then another, until the smallest doll is revealed.

We learned about God's character and goodness and then opened another layer to discover the gift of gratitude, which then revealed the gift of hope, and now the gift of faith. Each new discovery teaches us something about God, His Son, and our faith. Today's reading moves us from "what faith is" to "what faith does."

Our faith in Jesus and the power of the Holy Spirit gives us the boldness to approach God with the desires of our heart, trusting that His will is the right answer to what we need. The result of that faith is peace. No matter what circumstances we face, no matter how complicated or confusing life feels, when we have faith in God—believing that He is the creator and ruler of all—we can be at peace.

Peace isn't a feeling or an experience that only happens at Christmas with our "Peace on Earth" decorations. Peace is the result of the gift of faith that God has given us, and it's a gift we can share with others as we tell them why we celebrate Jesus and excitedly await His promised arrival.

PRAYER

God, thank You for so generously giving me every good and perfect gift that I need to grow in my faith and encourage others. The more I learn about You, the more in awe I am of the depth of Your love for me. Give me the opportunity to share the reason for my peace with others this Christmas. Amen.

WEEK 4
Thursday

READ

Ephesians 6:10–20

Finally, be strengthened in the Lord and in the strength of his power. 11 Clothe yourselves with the full armor of God, so that you will be able to stand against the schemes of the devil. 12 For our struggle is not against flesh and blood, but against the rulers, against the powers, against the world rulers of this darkness, against the spiritual forces of evil in the heavens.13 For this reason, take up the full armor of God so that you may be able to stand your ground on the evil day, and having done everything, to stand. 14 Stand firm therefore, by fastening the belt of truth around your waist, by putting on the breastplate of righteousness, 15 by fitting your feet with the preparation that comes from the good news of peace, 16 and in all of this, by taking up the shield of faith with which you can extinguish all the flaming arrows of the evil one. 17 And take *the helmet of salvation* and the sword of the Spirit (which is the word of God). 18 With every prayer and petition, pray at all times in the Spirit, and to this end be alert, with all perseverance and petitions for all the saints. 19 Pray for me also, that I may be given the right words when I begin to speak—that I may confidently make known the mystery of the gospel, 20 for which I am an ambassador in chains. Pray that I may be able to speak boldly as I ought to speak.

SOAP
WEEK 4 • THURSDAY

SOAP / *Ephesians 6:16*
SCRIPTURE / *Write out the SOAP verses*

OBSERVATION / *Write 3 - 4 observations*

APPLICATION / *Write down 1 - 2 applications*

PRAYER / *Write out a prayer over what you learned*

DEVOTIONAL
WEEK 4 • THURSDAY

SOAP

Ephesians 6:16

And in all of this, by taking up the shield of faith with which you can extinguish all the flaming arrows of the evil one.

INTO THE TEXT

In Paul's letter to the Ephesians and in his letter to the Thessalonians (1 Thessalonians 5:8–10), he gave the early church some very clear instructions to help them on their faith journey. He knew they needed more than a pat on the back and a reminder to "just have faith." This faith of ours sets us apart from the world. It requires endurance, steadfastness, love, and trust. But as disciple-makers, we are also called to action.

God provides full armor for us that we can put on, offering the protection of faith. The weapons of truth, righteousness, peace, faith, and salvation are meant for us to apply to our lives, to put into daily use. God's Word and prayer are essential weapons to combat the lies of the enemy. It is our very faith that protects us, and God has given us all the tools we need.

Through the gift of faith, God has equipped us to navigate all that we'll face in this world with confidence, knowing that our faith gives us hope, peace, and protection.

This is faith in action. This is preparing ourselves as the warrior daughters of the King, not worriers, ready and prepared to go to battle for our very souls. We are given the armor and the playbook, and God equips us to go and make disciples, to be the light, to serve His children with love while the enemy tries every sneak attack he knows.

PRAYER

Father, thank You for faith that protects and for all the tools You have given me to fight the battles and schemes of the enemy. As I wake each morning, help me remember to put on the armor You have given me so I can be prepared and protected to face each day with faith and trust in You. Amen.

WEEK 4
Friday

READ

Psalm 103
By David.

Praise the Lord, O my soul. With all that is within me, praise his holy name. 2 Praise the Lord, O my soul. Do not forget all his kind deeds. 3 He is the one who forgives all your sins, who heals all your diseases, 4 who delivers your life from the Pit, who crowns you with his loyal love and compassion, 5 who satisfies your life with good things, so your youth is renewed like an eagle's. 6 The Lord does what is fair, and executes justice for all the oppressed. 7 The Lord revealed his faithful acts to Moses, his deeds to the Israelites. 8 The Lord is compassionate and merciful; he is patient and demonstrates great loyal love. 9 He does not always accuse, and does not stay angry. 10 He does not deal with us as our sins deserve; he does not repay us as our misdeeds deserve. 11 For as the skies are high above the earth, so his loyal love towers over his faithful followers. 12 As far as the eastern horizon is from the west, so he removes the guilt of our rebellious actions from us. 13 As a father has compassion on his children, so the Lord has compassion on his faithful followers. 14 For he knows what we are made of; he realizes we are made of clay. 15 A person's life is like grass. Like a flower in the field it flourishes, 16 but when the hot wind blows, it disappears, and one can no longer even spot the place where it once grew. 17 But the Lord continually shows loyal love to his faithful followers, and is faithful to their descendants, 18 to those who keep his covenant, who are careful to obey his commands. 19 The Lord has established his throne in heaven; his kingdom extends over everything. 20 Praise the Lord, you angels of his, you powerful warriors who carry out his decrees and obey his orders. 21 Praise the Lord, all you warriors of his, you servants of his who carry out his desires. 22 Praise the Lord, all that he has made, in all the regions of his kingdom. Praise the Lord, O my soul.

SOAP

WEEK 4 · FRIDAY

SOAP / *Psalm 103:8–10*
SCRIPTURE / *Write out the SOAP verses*

OBSERVATION / *Write 3 - 4 observations*

APPLICATION / *Write down 1 - 2 applications*

PRAYER / *Write out a prayer over what you learned*

DEVOTIONAL
WEEK 4 • FRIDAY

SOAP

Psalm 103:8–10

The Lord is compassionate and merciful; he is patient and demonstrates great loyal love. He does not always accuse, and does not stay angry. He does not deal with us as our sins deserve; he does not repay us as our misdeeds deserve.

INTO THE TEXT

As we end this week of Advent, let's turn our attention back to praising God for who He is and what He has done for us. God is good, and He has given us the most amazing Gift in His Son, Jesus. Not only is He good, but today's Psalm reminds us that God is incredibly patient with us.

Throughout the Bible we read stories of men and women of great faith, who were often distracted, disobedient, or delayed acting on the direction God gave them. But God never waivers from His plan, and He shows great patience toward His chosen people.

The psalmist recalls God's great kindness, forgiveness, healing, deliverance, love, compassion, renewal, justice, faithfulness, mercy, and patience. God does not deal with us the way we deserve, but designed a plan of salvation that required sending His Son as the ultimate sacrifice. Jesus, the baby we celebrate at Christmas, came to take on the sins of the world—a promise God made and kept over thousands of years.

Praise God today for His patience in your life. Remember the times He waited for you, loved you, carried you, and kept His promises to you. This great gift of Jesus that we're about to celebrate was sent for you, long before you would ever make the decision to accept Him as your Savior. What a beautiful gift!

PRAYER

God, thank You for being incredibly, unbelievably patient with me. Help me to pass that gift along to others this Christmas season instead of choosing frustration or impatience. May my life be a reflection of Your character to those around me. Amen.

REFLECT

WEEK 4

1. According to Hebrews 11:6, what is necessary for us to have in order to please God? Why does this please Him?

   ....
   ....
   ....

2. Does your faith impact God's willingness to answer your prayers? Why or why not?

   ....
   ....
   ....

3. Jesus healed many people in the Gospels because of their faith. Does God still answer our prayers this way today? Why or why not?

   ....
   ....
   ....

4. How does faith allow you to combat the attacks of the enemy?

   ....
   ....
   ....

5. Praise God for the gift of faith today. Record your prayer of thanksgiving along with a declaration of your faith in Him.

   ....
   ....
   ....

JOURNAL
your thoughts

JOURNAL
your thoughts

WEEK 5

My brothers and sisters, consider it nothing but (joy) when you fall into all sorts of trials, because you know that the testing of your faith <u>produces endurance</u>. And let endurance have its perfect effect, so that you will be <u>perfect</u> and <u>complete</u>, not deficient in anything.

James 1:2-4

PRAY

Write down your prayer requests and praises for this week.

WEEKLY CHALLENGE

Reflect on James 1:2–4 this week. Why is it important for you to find joy in trials? Are trials always meant to test your faith? Why do we need endurance in our walk of faith?

WEEK 5
Monday

READ

Psalm 16
A prayer of David.

Protect me, O God, for I have taken shelter in you. 2 I say to the Lord, "You are the Lord, my only source of well-being." 3 As for God's chosen people who are in the land, and the leading officials I admired so much— 4 their troubles multiply; they desire other gods. I will not pour out drink offerings of blood to their gods, nor will I make vows in the name of their gods. 5 Lord, you give me stability and prosperity; you make my future secure. 6 It is as if I have been given fertile fields or received a beautiful tract of land. 7 I will praise the Lord who guides me; yes, during the night I reflect and learn. 8 I constantly trust in the Lord; because he is at my right hand, I will not be shaken. 9 So my heart rejoices and I am happy; my life is safe. 10 You will not abandon me to Sheol; you will not allow your faithful follower to see the Pit. 11 You lead me in the path of life. I experience absolute joy in your presence; you always give me sheer delight.

SOAP
WEEK 5 • MONDAY

SOAP / *Psalm 16:11*
SCRIPTURE / *Write out the SOAP verses*

OBSERVATION / *Write 3 - 4 observations*

APPLICATION / *Write down 1 - 2 applications*

PRAYER / *Write out a prayer over what you learned*

DEVOTIONAL
WEEK 5 • MONDAY

SOAP

Psalm 16:11

You lead me in the path of life. I experience absolute joy in your presence; you always give me sheer delight.

INTO THE TEXT

The dictionary defines joy as, "a source or cause of delight." I don't know about you, but I think that's a pretty great definition of Jesus! This week for our Advent study we will spend some time focusing on another great gift that God has given us—the gift of joy! Joy is the theme of the third week of Advent, and it's a time to celebrate the good news of the birth of Jesus—news that definitely brings us joy!

There are so many parts of the Christmas season that can be a temporary source of delight. Twinkling lights, a fresh coat of snow, presents for friends and family, even the simple smile of a stranger on a busy evening. But this week we celebrate a source of joy that is eternal! When God sent Jesus to earth to be the atoning sacrifice for our sins, it was a permanent, unchanging covenant that would bring us back into a relationship with Him.

Because God's character is unchanging, we can celebrate this Christmas knowing that our joy is found in the presence of God, which we can experience personally through our relationship with Jesus, the greatest present we have ever been given. The psalmist writes that he experiences absolute joy in the presence of God—it never fails!

What do you need to do this week to make sure that spending time with God is at the very top of your list? Where have all of the obligations of the Christmas season taken your attention away from the promised joy you can experience when you rest in God's presence?

PRAYER

God, thank You for giving me the gift of joy. As I count down the days to the celebration of Your Son's birth, help me share the reason for my joy with the people I meet each day, because Your Good News is for all people! Amen.

WEEK 5
Tuesday

READ

Philippians 1

From Paul and Timothy, slaves of Christ Jesus, to all the saints in Christ Jesus who are in Philippi, with the overseers and deacons. 2 Grace and peace to you from God our Father and the Lord Jesus Christ! 3 I thank my God every time I remember you. 4 I always pray with joy in my every prayer for all of you 5 because of your participation in the gospel from the first day until now. 6 For I am sure of this very thing, that the one who began a good work in you will perfect it until the day of Christ Jesus. 7 For it is right for me to think this about all of you, because I have you in my heart, since both in my imprisonment and in the defense and confirmation of the gospel all of you became partners in God's grace together with me. 8 For God is my witness that I long for all of you with the affection of Christ Jesus. 9 And I pray this, that your love may abound even more and more in knowledge and every kind of insight 10 so that you can decide what is best, and thus be sincere and blameless for the day of Christ, 11 filled with the fruit of righteousness that comes through Jesus Christ to the glory and praise of God. 12 I want you to know, brothers and sisters, that my situation has actually turned out to advance the gospel: 13 The whole imperial guard and everyone else knows that I am in prison for the sake of Christ, 14 and most of the brothers and sisters, having confidence in the Lord because of my imprisonment, now more than ever dare to speak the word fearlessly. 15 Some, to be sure, are preaching Christ from envy and rivalry, but others from goodwill. 16 The latter do so from love because they know that I am placed here for the defense of the gospel. 17 The former proclaim Christ from selfish ambition, not sincerely, because they think they can cause trouble for me in my imprisonment. 18 What is the result?

WEEK 5
Tuesday

Philippians 1 (continued)

Only that in every way, whether in pretense or in truth, Christ is being proclaimed, and in this I rejoice. Yes, and I will continue to rejoice, 19 for I know that this will turn out for my deliverance through your prayers and the help of the Spirit of Jesus Christ. 20 My confident hope is that I will in no way be ashamed but that with complete boldness, even now as always, Christ will be exalted in my body, whether I live or die. 21 For to me, living is Christ and dying is gain. 22 Now if I am to go on living in the body, this will mean productive work for me, yet I don't know which I prefer: 23 I feel torn between the two, because I have a desire to depart and be with Christ, which is better by far, 24 but it is more vital for your sake that I remain in the body. 25 And since I am sure of this, I know that I will remain and continue with all of you for the sake of your progress and joy in the faith, 26 so that what you can be proud of may increase because of me in Christ Jesus, when I come back to you. 27 Only conduct yourselves in a manner worthy of the gospel of Christ so that—whether I come and see you or whether I remain absent—I should hear that you are standing firm in one spirit, with one mind, by contending side by side for the faith of the gospel, 28 and by not being intimidated in any way by your opponents. This is a sign of their destruction, but of your salvation—a sign which is from God. 29 For it has been granted to you not only to believe in Christ but also to suffer for him, 30 since you are encountering the same conflict that you saw me face and now hear that I am facing.

James 1:2–4

My brothers and sisters, consider it nothing but joy when you fall into all sorts of trials, 3 because you know that the testing of your faith produces endurance. 4 And let endurance have its perfect effect, so that you will be perfect and complete, not deficient in anything.

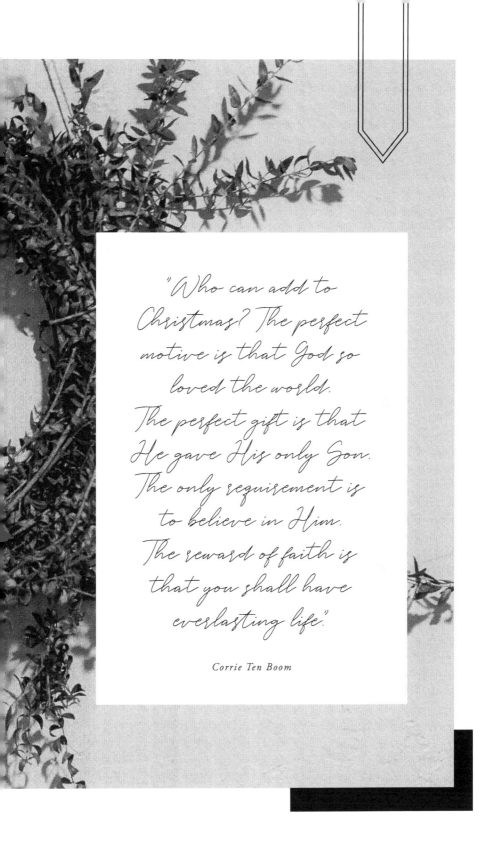

"Who can add to Christmas? The perfect motive is that God so loved the world. The perfect gift is that He gave His only Son. The only requirement is to believe in Him. The reward of faith is that you shall have everlasting life."

Corrie Ten Boom

SOAP

WEEK 5 · TUESDAY

SOAP / *James 1:2–4*
SCRIPTURE / *Write out the SOAP verses*

OBSERVATION / *Write 3 - 4 observations*

APPLICATION / *Write down 1 - 2 applications*

PRAYER / *Write out a prayer over what you learned*

DEVOTIONAL
WEEK 5 • TUESDAY

SOAP

James 1:2–4

My brothers and sisters, consider it nothing but joy when you fall into all sorts of trials, because you know that the testing of your faith produces endurance. And let endurance have its perfect effect, so that you will be perfect and complete, not deficient in anything.

INTO THE TEXT

Life is a complicated mix of ups and downs, highs and lows, mountain tops and valleys. In our passage today, James is writing to the early church to encourage them that, no matter what trials they faced, there was joy to be found—and that same encouragement applies to us, too!

How do we experience joy even through trials? As believers, we know our current circumstances are temporary and that we have a perfect home in heaven waiting for us. When we move our focus away from what is happening to us and around us and instead turn our focus up to God, we can look for the lessons to be learned along the way.

James tells us that the testing of our faith produces endurance, or the ability to endure with patience. As our endurance is developed, our faith is strengthened, which results in our lives being "perfect and complete." In this case, perfect does not mean that we won't make mistakes or experience future trials, but our faith will be mature, complete, and whole.

God has given us the gift of joy, which we can find in His presence and in our relationship with Jesus. Our circumstances are not our source of joy, but we can choose to live out our faith through all seasons, the easy and the hard, the good and the bad, with a desire to become more like Christ. It will be our example in those challenging times, when others continue to see us find joy in the trials, that might be the greatest gift we can give them.

PRAYER

Father, it doesn't make sense that I would find joy in our trials, but Your ways are so much greater than the ways of the world. Thank You for giving me the gift of joy and an eternal focus that helps me persevere and grow in endurance as my faith is strengthened. Amen.

WEEK 5
Wednesday

READ

Psalm 30
A psalm, a song used at the dedication
of the temple; by David.

I will praise you, O Lord, for you lifted me up, and did not allow my enemies to gloat over me. 2 O Lord my God, I cried out to you and you healed me. 3 O Lord, you pulled me up from Sheol; you rescued me from among those descending into the grave. 4 Sing to the Lord, you faithful followers of his; give thanks to his holy name. 5 For his anger lasts only a brief moment, and his good favor restores one's life. One may experience sorrow during the night, but joy arrives in the morning. 6 In my self-confidence I said, "I will never be shaken." 7 O Lord, in your good favor you made me secure. Then you rejected me and I was terrified. 8 To you, O Lord, I cried out; I begged the Lord for mercy: 9 "What profit is there in taking my life, in my descending into the Pit? Can the dust of the grave praise you? Can it declare your loyalty? 10 Hear, O Lord, and have mercy on me. O Lord, deliver me." 11 Then you turned my lament into dancing; you removed my sackcloth and covered me with joy. 12 So now my heart will sing to you and not be silent; O Lord my God, I will always give thanks to you.

SOAP

WEEK 5 • WEDNESDAY

SOAP / *Psalm 30:11–12*
SCRIPTURE / *Write out the SOAP verses*

OBSERVATION / *Write 3 - 4 observations*

APPLICATION / *Write down 1 - 2 applications*

PRAYER / *Write out a prayer over what you learned*

DEVOTIONAL
WEEK 5 • WEDNESDAY

SOAP

Psalm 30:11–12

Then you turned my lament into dancing; you removed my sackcloth and covered me with joy. So now my heart will sing to you and not be silent; O Lord my God, I will always give thanks to you.

INTO THE TEXT

When was the last time you allowed yourself to feel truly joyful? Imagine the last time you closed your eyes, hands lifted toward the heavens, a beautiful smile on your face, and your heart full of laughter. Your heart felt full of wonder and delight and your feet couldn't help dancing, just a little bit.

What if you were to give yourself permission to come before God like that today? For just ten minutes, let the burdens and heaviness of the year fall at the foot of the cross and joyfully worship God. Laugh, sing, dance, smile—let yourself become a child again in the presence of your Father. Trust that He welcomes your praise and has given you the gift of joy so you can experience it fully and deeply. Not only that, God wants to exchange your sadness for joy and your silence for singing!

Put on your favorite upbeat worship or Christmas music and enjoy this moment with God, worshipping Him for all that He is, all that He has given you, and all that He promises to do in the future. At Christmas, we celebrate the birth of the Savior of the world, and God is not done giving His children good gifts. Take a moment away from the busyness and simply worship God, experiencing the joy that comes from being fully in His presence.

PRAYER

God, You alone are worthy of our praise. Thank You for the glorious exchange of my mourning for joy, my silence for singing. Today I place my burdens in Your capable hands and willingly exchange them for the joy You promise. I will give You thanks forever and ever. Amen.

WEEK 5
Thursday

READ

John 16:19–24

Jesus could see that they wanted to ask him about these things, so he said to them, "Are you asking each other about this—that I said, 'In a little while you will not see me; again after a little while, you will see me'? 20 I tell you the solemn truth, you will weep and wail, but the world will rejoice; you will be sad, but your sadness will turn into joy. 21 When a woman gives birth, she has distress because her time has come, but when her child is born, she no longer remembers the suffering because of her joy that a human being has been born into the world. 22 So also you have sorrow now, but *I will see you again, and your hearts will rejoice, and no one will take your joy away from you.* 23 At that time you will ask me nothing. I tell you the solemn truth, whatever you ask the Father in my name he will give you. 24 Until now you have not asked for anything in my name. Ask and you will receive it, so that your joy may be complete.

SOAP
WEEK 5 • THURSDAY

SOAP / *John 16:22*
SCRIPTURE / *Write out the SOAP verses*

OBSERVATION / *Write 3 - 4 observations*

APPLICATION / *Write down 1 - 2 applications*

PRAYER / *Write out a prayer over what you learned*

DEVOTIONAL
WEEK 5 • THURSDAY

SOAP

John 16:22

So also you have sorrow now, but I will see you again, and your hearts will rejoice, and no one will take your joy away from you.

INTO THE TEXT

Jesus made a promise to His disciples that continues to bring us great joy today. The disciples were chatting with one another, off to the side, and Jesus answered a question they had not actually asked Him directly. Jesus had told them that He would go and come again, and they were struggling to understand what He meant. Although Jesus would be crucified and die, He would return to see them again. And He did! One day, we will also see Jesus return, but until that day we can find joy knowing that "Promise-Keeper" is an unchanging characteristic of our God.

In our verses today, Jesus told the disciples that, although they were experiencing sorrow because He was going to leave them, with a change in perspective and focus, those same circumstances filled them with joy. When we change our perspective, our sorrows can actually become our joy, our reason for rejoicing. The things that cause us pain become the avenues God uses to bring lasting joy into our lives.

Jesus is a promise kept. His birth, every detail of it, was planned and prophesied and perfectly orchestrated so that there would be no doubt that He was the promised Messiah. Jesus' death and resurrection completed another part of the promise, and we can find joy as we celebrate that no scheme of humans will ever ruin what God has put into motion. We will see Jesus again, and no one can take that joy from us!

PRAYER

Heavenly Father, thank You for so carefully and thoughtfully planning every part of the promise You made to send us a Redeemer. May my joy be found in You alone, knowing that sorrow is temporary but the joy is eternal. Amen.

WEEK 5
Friday

READ

Psalm 147

Praise the LORD, for it is good to sing praises to our God. Yes, praise is pleasant and appropriate. 2 The LORD rebuilds Jerusalem, and gathers the exiles of Israel. 3 He heals the brokenhearted, and bandages their wounds. 4 He counts the number of the stars; he names all of them. 5 Our LORD is great and has awesome power; there is no limit to his wisdom. 6 The LORD lifts up the oppressed, but knocks the wicked to the ground. 7 Offer to the LORD a song of thanks. Sing praises to our God to the accompaniment of a harp. 8 He covers the sky with clouds, provides the earth with rain, and causes grass to grow on the hillsides. 9 He gives food to the animals, and to the young ravens when they chirp. 10 He is not enamored with the strength of a horse, nor is he impressed by the warrior's strong legs. 11 The LORD takes delight in his faithful followers, and in those who wait for his loyal love. 12 Extol the LORD, O Jerusalem. Praise your God, O Zion. 13 For he makes the bars of your gates strong. He blesses your children within you. 14 He brings peace to your territory. He abundantly provides for you the best grain. 15 He sends his command through the earth; swiftly his order reaches its destination. 16 He sends the snow that is white like wool; he spreads the frost that is white like ashes. 17 He throws his hailstones like crumbs. Who can withstand the cold wind he sends? 18 He then orders it all to melt; he breathes on it, and the water flows. 19 He proclaims his word to Jacob, his statutes and regulations to Israel. 20 He has not done so with any other nation; they are not aware of his regulations. Praise the LORD!

SOAP

WEEK 5 • FRIDAY

SOAP / *Psalm 147:1*
SCRIPTURE / *Write out the SOAP verses*

OBSERVATION / *Write 3 - 4 observations*

APPLICATION / *Write down 1 - 2 applications*

PRAYER / *Write out a prayer over what you learned*

DEVOTIONAL
WEEK 5 · FRIDAY

SOAP

Psalm 147:1

Praise the LORD, for it is good to sing praises to our God. Yes, praise is pleasant and appropriate.

INTO THE TEXT

The Christmas season can be a difficult time for many of us. Some are facing a first Christmas without a loved one, or distance has made it impossible to gather together. Maybe Christmas was a hard season when you were growing up and the traditions and activities only bring back discouraging memories.

If any part of your heart feels broken today, let our Scripture be a gentle reminder that God will be there to heal and repair your spirit, the same way He was there for the Israelites long ago. The very same God who created, numbered, and named every star in the sky knows your name. You are beautifully created in His image, and there is no part of your past, present, or future that He does not care about.

It is good to sing praises about God! Consider all of the gifts we have learned about so far in this Advent study, and all the little ways God cares about you. It is good to praise God about those things, because it helps lift our minds and change our focus. When we feel like the pressure of the holidays is too much, take some time to think on things that are good and worthy of praise (Philippians 4:8).

Praise is pleasant and appropriate. It honors God and it's good for our hearts, too. As God's chosen people, we have the distinct privilege of being invited to come before His throne with boldness. Let's spend that time in praise today!

PRAYER

God, You know me better than I know myself. Thank You for being near when I'm brokenhearted, comforting me when I need You most, and never leaving me. It is a gift to be able to praise Your holy name. Amen.

REFLECT

WEEK 5

1. Why is joy found in God's presence? What emotions do you experience as you spend time with God?

....
....
....

2. How can you find joy in trials? How do trials lead to endurance in your faith?

....
....
....

3. Have you experienced what the Psalmist talks about in Psalm 30:11–12? Has there been a time in your life when God has turned your lament into joy?

....
....
....

4. If you are in Christ, no one and nothing can take your joy. How does this truth give you comfort?

....
....
....

5. What has brought you joy this week? Praise God for these things today.

....
....
....

JOURNAL
your thoughts

JOURNAL
your thoughts

WEEK 6

And the peace of God that surpasses all understanding will guard your hearts and minds in Christ Jesus.

Philippians 4:7

PRAY

Write down your prayer requests and praises for this week.

....
....
....
....
....
....
....
....
....
....
....
....
....
....

WEEKLY CHALLENGE

In Philippians 4:6–8, Paul tells his readers that the peace of Christ guards our hearts. How does meditating on things that are true, worthy of respect, just, pure, lovely, commendable, excellent, or praiseworthy guard our hearts and minds? This week, take time to evaluate your thoughts, making sure to focus on things that match this list.

....
....
....
....
....
....
....

WEEK 6

Monday

READ

Colossians 3:12–17

Therefore, as the elect of God, holy and dearly loved, clothe yourselves with a heart of mercy, kindness, humility, gentleness, and patience, 13 bearing with one another and forgiving one another, if someone happens to have a complaint against anyone else. Just as the Lord has forgiven you, so you also forgive others. 14 And to all these virtues add love, which is the perfect bond. 15 Let the peace of Christ be in control in your heart (for you were in fact called as one body to this peace), and be thankful. 16 Let the word of Christ dwell in you richly, teaching and exhorting one another with all wisdom, singing psalms, hymns, and spiritual songs, all with grace in your hearts to God. 17 And whatever you do in word or deed, do it all in the name of the Lord Jesus, giving thanks to God the Father through him.

SOAP

WEEK 6 · MONDAY

SOAP / *Colossians 3:15*
SCRIPTURE / *Write out the SOAP verses*

OBSERVATION / *Write 3 - 4 observations*

APPLICATION / *Write down 1 - 2 applications*

PRAYER / *Write out a prayer over what you learned*

DEVOTIONAL
WEEK 6 • MONDAY

SOAP

Colossians 3:15

Let the peace of Christ be in control in your heart (for you were in fact called as one body to this peace), and be thankful.

INTO THE TEXT

As we begin our final week of our Advent study and Christmas Day draws near, it feels fitting that we spend some time studying peace. We read in the account of Jesus' birth in Luke that the shepherds were visited by an angel and great heavenly army singing, "Glory to God in the highest, and on earth peace among people with whom he is pleased!" (Luke 2:14). While shepherds and wise men brought gifts to Jesus, He brought us the gift of peace.

This peace isn't a feeling, but a daily choice to let Christ be in control of our hearts. Each morning we are called to put on a very specific outfit: mercy, kindness, humility, gentleness, patience, forgiveness, and love (Colossians 3:12–14). This is the outward showing of what God is doing in our hearts, and when we choose to add these characteristics and behaviors, we can be people who live in peace with others.

Once we have clothed ourselves in these virtues, we can stand firm in our faith when we "Let the word of Christ dwell in you richly, teaching and exhorting one another with all wisdom, singing psalms, hymns, and spiritual songs, all with grace in your hearts to God" (Colossians 3:16). Living in peace with other believers happens best when we work on it together, holding one another accountable to our time in the Word, when we share what God is doing in our lives, when we encourage one another, and when we praise God together.

We are called to be ambassadors of Christ who show the world what peace on earth can truly look like. How can you share this peace with others this week?

PRAYER

God, thank You for the great gift of Jesus and the peace He made available for each of us. Help me choose each day to clothe myself in the virtues and behaviors that bring You glory and encourage others to live in peace. Amen.

WEEK 6
Tuesday

READ

Philippians 4:2–9

I appeal to Euodia and to Syntyche to agree in the Lord. 3 Yes, I say also to you, true companion, help them. They have struggled together in the gospel ministry along with me and Clement and my other coworkers, whose names are in the book of life. 4 Rejoice in the Lord always. Again I say, rejoice! 5 Let everyone see your gentleness. The Lord is near! 6 Do not be anxious about anything. Instead, in every situation, through prayer and petition with thanksgiving, tell your requests to God. 7 And the peace of God that surpasses all understanding will guard your hearts and minds in Christ Jesus. 8 Finally, brothers and sisters, whatever is true, whatever is worthy of respect, whatever is just, whatever is pure, whatever is lovely, whatever is commendable, if something is excellent or praiseworthy, think about these things. 9 And what you learned and received and heard and saw in me, do these things. And the God of peace will be with you.

SOAP

WEEK 6 · TUESDAY

SOAP / *Philippians 4:6–8*
SCRIPTURE / *Write out the SOAP verses*

OBSERVATION / *Write 3 - 4 observations*

APPLICATION / *Write down 1 - 2 applications*

PRAYER / *Write out a prayer over what you learned*

DEVOTIONAL
WEEK 6 • TUESDAY

SOAP

Philippians 4:6–8

Do not be anxious about anything. Instead, in every situation, through prayer and petition with thanksgiving, tell your requests to God. And the peace of God that surpasses all understanding will guard your hearts and minds in Christ Jesus. Finally, brothers and sisters, whatever is true, whatever is worthy of respect, whatever is just, whatever is pure, whatever is lovely, whatever is commendable, if something is excellent or praiseworthy, think about these things.

INTO THE TEXT

Have you ever wondered why it's so hard to change how we think about things—about our lives, our circumstances, and ourselves? Scripture tells us that our words are an overflow of our hearts (Luke 6:45). How we speak, to others and to ourselves, is a reflection of what is in our hearts. Our thoughts follow our hearts, and our words follow our thoughts. Maybe you've heard it like this: garbage in, garbage out.

When it comes to our faith lives, hearts filled with God, grace, and the gospel bear good fruit in thought, word, and action. Hearts that are focused on the expectations and demands of the world will bear bad fruit. Through salvation and with God's help, we can be, as it says in Romans 12:2, transformed by the renewing of our minds.

And that transformation can make the difference between surviving and thriving. It's been said that Satan doesn't need to destroy us, only distract us, to keep us from fulfilling the plans God has for us. What better way than to distract us with the noise of the world, filling our hearts and minds with all the things we think we should be doing, but then missing out on the fulfilling work God has for us?

Science tells us that our thoughts create patterns in our brains that change the landscape of our brains, cells, and genes. As thoughts travel, they create pathways that create habits. Science and Scripture agree, however, that we can actually change our minds! With God, we can change the direction of our thoughts. It's not impossible, but we can't do it on our own. All of the anxious thoughts need to be torn down to make room so we can abide with Jesus, serving His kingdom with confidence and peace.

PRAYER

God, thank You for giving me a way to change my mind so that my thoughts go toward things that are true and praiseworthy. Help me develop a habit of prayer so my worries and anxious thoughts can find peace in Your presence. Amen.

WEEK 6
Wednesday

READ

Isaiah 26:3

You keep completely safe the people who maintain their faith, for they trust in you.

2 Corinthians 1:3–11

Blessed is the God and Father of our Lord Jesus Christ, the Father of mercies and God of all comfort, 4 who comforts us in all our troubles so that we may be able to comfort those experiencing any trouble with the comfort with which we ourselves are comforted by God. 5 For just as the sufferings of Christ overflow toward us, so also our comfort through Christ overflows to you. 6 But if we are afflicted, it is for your comfort and salvation; if we are comforted, it is for your comfort that you experience in your patient endurance of the same sufferings that we also suffer. 7 And our hope for you is steadfast because we know that as you share in our sufferings, so also you will share in our comfort. 8 For we do not want you to be unaware, brothers and sisters, regarding the affliction that happened to us in the province of Asia, that we were burdened excessively, beyond our strength, so that we despaired even of living. 9 Indeed we felt as if the sentence of death had been passed against us, so that we would not trust in ourselves but in God who raises the dead. 10 He delivered us from so great a risk of death, and he will deliver us. We have set our hope on him that he will deliver us yet again, 11 as you also join in helping us by prayer, so that many people may give thanks to God on our behalf for the gracious gift given to us through the help of many.

SOAP

WEEK 6 • WEDNESDAY

SOAP / *Isaiah 26:3*
SCRIPTURE / *Write out the SOAP verses*

OBSERVATION / *Write 3 - 4 observations*

APPLICATION / *Write down 1 - 2 applications*

PRAYER / *Write out a prayer over what you learned*

DEVOTIONAL
WEEK 6 • WEDNESDAY

SOAP

Isaiah 26:3

You keep completely safe the people who maintain their faith, for they trust in you.

INTO THE TEXT

We have learned through our study that God is good, and He is consistent and unchanging. But our God is also just, and the prophet Isaiah had some hard words to share with those who would defy the covenant God made with His people. But for those who remain faithful, God promises peace and safety.

In chapter 26, Isaiah shifts our attention from the circumstances of the fallen world around us back up to the perfect kingdom of heaven. Although we have yet to see it, we can take heart knowing that God will do what He says He will do: our God will reign over all. No matter what happens in the world, in our communities, or in our families, God will have the final victory.

At Christmas we celebrate the arrival of Jesus, our Savior, as a baby born of a virgin, both God and man. But the story is just beginning, because we now get to live with the holy expectation of Christ's return—not as a baby, but our ultimate Deliverer.

As our faith becomes more steadfast and we hold on to the gifts and promises of God, we will experience peace, regardless of our circumstances.

PRAYER

God, You are my rock and my sure foundation. When I seek safety and peace, may I find it in Your presence, no matter my circumstances. Thank You for this gift of peace, and for always keeping Your promises. Amen.

WEEK 6
Thursday

READ

Isaiah 9:6

For a child has been born to us, a son has been given to us. He shoulders responsibility and is called Wonderful Adviser, Mighty God, Everlasting Father, Prince of Peace.

John 14:27–31

"Peace I leave with you; my peace I give to you; I do not give it to you as the world does. Do not let your hearts be distressed or lacking in courage. 28 You heard me say to you, 'I am going away and I am coming back to you.' If you loved me, you would be glad that I am going to the Father, because the Father is greater than I am. 29 I have told you now before it happens, so that when it happens you may believe. 30 I will not speak with you much longer, for the ruler of this world is coming. He has no power over me, 31 but I am doing just what the Father commanded me, so that the world may know that I love the Father. Get up, let us go from here.

SOAP

WEEK 6 · THURSDAY

SOAP / *John 14:27*
SCRIPTURE / *Write out the SOAP verses*

OBSERVATION / *Write 3 - 4 observations*

APPLICATION / *Write down 1 - 2 applications*

PRAYER / *Write out a prayer over what you learned*

DEVOTIONAL
WEEK 6 • THURSDAY

SOAP

John 14:27

Peace I leave with you; my peace I give to you; I do not give it to you as the world does. Do not let your hearts be distressed or lacking in courage.

INTO THE TEXT

God, our great Giver, gave us the most amazing Gift when He sent His Son to earth as our Redeemer. But in His great mercy and wisdom, God continues to give us good and perfect gifts, not just for today, but for our future.

The disciples had not yet realized the fullness of who Jesus was at this point in John's Gospel. They struggled to understand what Jesus was talking about when He said that He would be leaving to make a place for them in His Father's house. It is because of what Jesus would do on the cross that the disciples, and all who believe in Jesus, would no longer be separated from God.

In addition to this amazing gift, Jesus also promised to send a Helper, or the Holy Spirit, to be with us forever. It is only through the birth, death, and resurrection of Christ that we can have access to the Holy Spirit, access to God, access to the resources of heaven, an abundant life on earth, and an eternal life in heaven! Jesus also promises peace, not only for the time when the disciples were physically with Him, but peace for each of us that endures forever.

PRAYER

God, thank You for the gift of peace that You have given me, peace for today and for the future. I am so grateful that You do not give as the world gives, Your gifts are exactly what I need, not just what I want. Amen.

WEEK 6
Friday

READ

Psalm 113

Praise the Lord. Praise, you servants of the Lord, praise the name of the Lord. 2 May the Lord's name be praised now and forevermore. 3 From east to west the Lord's name is deserving of praise. 4 The Lord is exalted over all the nations; his splendor reaches beyond the sky. 5 Who can compare to the Lord our God, who sits on a high throne? 6 He bends down to look at the sky and the earth. 7 He raises the poor from the dirt, and lifts up the needy from the garbage pile, 8 that he might seat him with princes, with the princes of his people. 9 He makes the barren woman of the family a happy mother of children. Praise the Lord.

Luke 1:46–55

And Mary said, "My soul exalts the Lord, 47 and my spirit has begun to rejoice in God my Savior, 48 because he has looked upon the humble state of his servant. For from now on all generations will call me blessed, 49 because he who is mighty has done great things for me, and holy is his name; 50 from generation to generation he is merciful to those who fear him. 51 He has demonstrated power with his arm; he has scattered those whose pride wells up from the sheer arrogance of their hearts. 52 He has brought down the mighty from their thrones, and has lifted up those of lowly position; 53 he has filled the hungry with good things, and has sent the rich away empty. 54 He has helped his servant Israel, remembering his mercy, 55 as he promised to our ancestors, to Abraham and to his descendants forever."

SOAP

WEEK 6 • FRIDAY

SOAP / *Psalm 113:1–2*
SCRIPTURE / *Write out the SOAP verses*

OBSERVATION / *Write 3 - 4 observations*

APPLICATION / *Write down 1 - 2 applications*

PRAYER / *Write out a prayer over what you learned*

DEVOTIONAL
WEEK 6 · FRIDAY

SOAP

Psalm 113:1–2

Praise the LORD. Praise, you servants of the LORD, praise the name of the LORD. May the LORD's name be praised now and forevermore.

INTO THE TEXT

Today is a day for great celebration! Our Savior has arrived—the King of kings and Lord of lords! Our Redeemer has been born and we get to join with angels in heaven as we sing His praises. Before the gifts are opened, before the meals are shared, before the carols are sung, sing praise to God, for He alone is worthy.

Praise God for the gifts of hope, faith, joy, and peace that He has given us. Praise Him for the glorious gift of His Son, Jesus. Praise Him for all that He has done and for the accounts in Scripture that tell of His goodness, mercy, and love. Praise God for all He has done in your life, sing back to Him the story He has written in your life. Praise Him for the ways He has saved you, helped you, rescued you, loved you, healed you, redeemed you, and swapped sorrow for joy.

Praise God for loving us so much that He would do anything, across thousands of years, in the lives of countless men and women, to make His plan for our salvation work out perfectly. Praise Him that the salvation He offers is a gift, not something we can earn or work for, but a gift that is freely given.

Praise Him, like Mary, "because he who is mighty has done great things for me, and holy is his name" (Luke 1:49). Rejoice, friends! Today we celebrate the birth of Jesus—the greatest Gift given by our good and perfect Giver.

PRAYER

God, all of Your gifts are good and perfect. Thank You for sending Your Son to save us and for offering each of us the opportunity to accept your free gift of salvation. Thank You for the gifts of hope, faith, joy, and peace that You have given us—gifts for today, and for eternity. Amen.

REFLECT
WEEK 6

1. Is the peace of Christ in control in your heart? How can you allow this peace to have control of your heart, your mind, and your life?

   ....
   ....
   ....

2. How does God keep you safe? How does knowing He keeps you safe bring you peace?

   ....
   ....
   ....

3. What does it mean that Christ has given you His peace?

   ....
   ....
   ....

4. How does the peace of Christ guard you from becoming distressed or lacking courage?

   ....
   ....
   ....

5. How have you experienced the peace of God this week? Praise Him for His peace today.

   ....
   ....
   ....

JOURNAL
your thoughts

JOURNAL
your thoughts

Bri

BRIDGE

SOAP it up between studies
2 week reading plan

Have you developed a consistent, daily Bible study habit and don't want to break it before our next study begins? In the following pages, you can continue your quiet time with our suggested reading and SOAP passages.

READING PLAN

WEEK 1

- *Monday*
  Read: Psalm 131–132
  SOAP: Psalm 132:11–12
- *Tuesday*
  Read: Psalm 133–134
  SOAP: Psalm 133:1–2
- *Wednesday*
  Read: Psalm 135–136
  SOAP: Psalm 136:1
- *Thursday*
  Read: Psalm 137–138
  SOAP: Psalm 138:7–8
- *Friday*
  Read: Psalm 139–140
  SOAP: Psalm 139:23–34

WEEK 2

- *Monday*
  Read: Psalm 141–142
  SOAP: Psalm 141:3–4
- *Tuesday*
  Read: Psalm 143–144
  SOAP: Psalm 144:1–2
- *Wednesday*
  Read: Psalm 145–146
  SOAP: Psalm 145:17–21
- *Thursday*
  Read: Psalm 147–148
  SOAP: Psalm 147:11
- *Friday*
  Read: Psalm 149–150
  SOAP: Psalm 149:4–5

BRIDGE / WEEK 1

Give thanks to the Lord, for he is good, for his loyal love endures.

Psalm 136:1

PRAY

Write down your prayer requests and praises for this week.

WEEK 1
Monday

READ

Psalm 131
A song of ascents, by David.

O Lord, my heart is not proud, nor do I have a haughty look. I do not have great aspirations, or concern myself with things that are beyond me. 2 Indeed, I have calmed and quieted myself like a weaned child with its mother; I am content like a young child. 3 O Israel, hope in the Lord now and forevermore!

Psalm 132
A song of ascents.

O Lord, for David's sake remember all his strenuous effort, 2 and how he made a vow to the Lord, and swore an oath to the Powerful One of Jacob. 3 He said, "I will not enter my own home, or get into my bed. 4 I will not allow my eyes to sleep, or my eyelids to slumber, 5 until I find a place for the Lord, a fine dwelling place for the Powerful One of Jacob." 6 Look, we heard about it in Ephrathah; we found it in the territory of Jaar. 7 Let us go to his dwelling place. Let us worship before his footstool. 8 Ascend, O Lord, to your resting place, you and the ark of your strength. 9 May your priests be clothed with integrity. May your loyal followers shout for joy. 10 For the sake of David, your servant, do not reject your chosen king. 11 The Lord made a reliable promise to David; he will not go back on his word. He said, "I will place one of your descendants on your throne. 12 If your sons keep my covenant and the rules I teach them, their sons will also sit on your throne forever." 13 Certainly the Lord has chosen Zion; he decided to make it his home. 14 He said, "This will be my resting place forever; I will live here, for I have chosen it. 15 I will abundantly supply what she needs; I will give her poor all the food they need. 16 I will protect her priests, and her godly people will shout exuberantly. 17 There I will make David strong; I have determined that my chosen king's dynasty will continue. 18 I will humiliate his enemies, and his crown will shine."

SOAP

WEEK 1 • MONDAY

SOAP / *Psalm 132:11–12*
SCRIPTURE / *Write out the SOAP verses*

OBSERVATION / *Write 3 - 4 observations*

APPLICATION / *Write down 1 - 2 applications*

PRAYER / *Write out a prayer over what you learned*

THANKFUL

WEEK 1 • MONDAY

*Write three things you are thankful for today
and why each one brings you joy.*

ONE

....
....
....
....
....
....
....
....

TWO

....
....
....
....
....
....
....
....

THREE

....
....
....
....
....
....
....
....

WEEK 1

Tuesday

READ

Psalm 133
A song of ascents; by David.

Look! How good and how pleasant it is when brothers truly live in unity. 2 It is like fine oil poured on the head, which flows down the beard— Aaron's beard, and then flows down his garments. 3 It is like the dew of Hermon, which flows down upon the hills of Zion. Indeed, that is where the Lord has decreed a blessing will be available—eternal life.

Psalm 134
A song of ascents.

Attention! Praise the Lord, all you servants of the Lord, who serve in the Lord's temple during the night. 2 Lift your hands toward the sanctuary and praise the Lord. 3 May the Lord, the Creator of heaven and earth, bless you from Zion.

SOAP
WEEK 1 • TUESDAY

SOAP / *Psalm 133:1–2*
SCRIPTURE / *Write out the SOAP verses*

OBSERVATION / *Write 3 - 4 observations*

APPLICATION / *Write down 1 - 2 applications*

PRAYER / *Write out a prayer over what you learned*

THANKFUL
WEEK 1 • TUESDAY

Write three things you are thankful for today and why each one brings you joy.

ONE

....
....
....
....
....
....
....

TWO

....
....
....
....
....
....
....

THREE

....
....
....
....
....
....
....

WEEK 1
Wednesday

READ

Psalm 135

Praise the Lord. Praise the name of the Lord. Offer praise, you servants of the Lord, 2 who serve in the Lord's temple, in the courts of the temple of our God. 3 Praise the Lord, for the Lord is good. Sing praises to his name, for it is pleasant. 4 Indeed, the Lord has chosen Jacob for himself, Israel to be his special possession. 5 Yes, I know the Lord is great, and our Lord is superior to all gods. 6 He does whatever he pleases in heaven and on earth, in the seas and all the ocean depths. 7 He causes the clouds to arise from the end of the earth, makes lightning bolts accompany the rain, and brings the wind out of his storehouses. 8 He struck down the firstborn of Egypt, including both men and animals. 9 He performed awesome deeds and acts of judgment in your midst, O Egypt, against Pharaoh and all his servants. 10 He defeated many nations, and killed mighty kings— 11 Sihon, king of the Amorites, and Og, king of Bashan, and all the kingdoms of Canaan. 12 He gave their land as an inheritance, as an inheritance to Israel his people. 13 O Lord, your name endures, your reputation, O Lord, lasts. 14 For the Lord vindicates his people, and has compassion on his servants. 15 The nations' idols are made of silver and gold; they are man-made. 16 They have mouths, but cannot speak, eyes, but cannot see, 17 and ears, but cannot hear. Indeed, they cannot breathe. 18 Those who make them will end up like them, as will everyone who trusts in them. 19 O family of Israel, praise the Lord. O family of Aaron, praise the Lord. 20 O family of Levi, praise the Lord. You loyal followers of the Lord, praise the Lord. 21 The Lord deserves praise in Zion— he who dwells in Jerusalem. Praise the Lord.

WEEK 1

Wednesday

Psalm 136

Give thanks to the Lord, for he is good, for his loyal love endures. 2 Give thanks to the God of gods, for his loyal love endures. 3 Give thanks to the Lord of lords, for his loyal love endures, 4 to the one who performs magnificent, amazing deeds all by himself, for his loyal love endures, 5 to the one who used wisdom to make the heavens, for his loyal love endures, 6 to the one who spread out the earth over the water, for his loyal love endures, 7 to the one who made the great lights, for his loyal love endures, 8 the sun to rule by day, for his loyal love endures, 9 the moon and stars to rule by night, for his loyal love endures, 10 to the one who struck down the firstborn of Egypt, for his loyal love endures, 11 and led Israel out from their midst, for his loyal love endures, 12 with a strong hand and an outstretched arm, for his loyal love endures, 13 to the one who divided the Red Sea in two, for his loyal love endures, 14 and led Israel through its midst, for his loyal love endures, 15 and tossed Pharaoh and his army into the Red Sea, for his loyal love endures, 16 to the one who led his people through the wilderness, for his loyal love endures, 17 to the one who struck down great kings, for his loyal love endures, 18 and killed powerful kings, for his loyal love endures, 19 Sihon, king of the Amorites, for his loyal love endures, 20 Og, king of Bashan, for his loyal love endures, 21 and gave their land as an inheritance, for his loyal love endures, 22 as an inheritance to Israel his servant, for his loyal love endures, 23 to the one who remembered us when we were down, for his loyal love endures, 24 and snatched us away from our enemies, for his loyal love endures, 25 to the one who gives food to all living things, for his loyal love endures. 26 Give thanks to the God of heaven, for his loyal love endures!

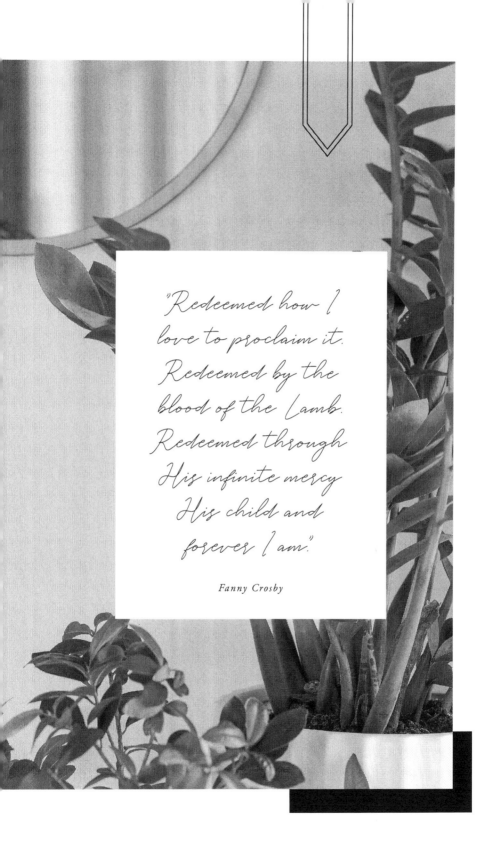

"Redeemed how I love to proclaim it. Redeemed by the blood of the Lamb. Redeemed through His infinite mercy His child and forever I am."

Fanny Crosby

SOAP

WEEK 1 • WEDNESDAY

SOAP / *Psalm 136:1*
SCRIPTURE / *Write out the SOAP verses*

OBSERVATION / *Write 3 - 4 observations*

APPLICATION / *Write down 1 - 2 applications*

PRAYER / *Write out a prayer over what you learned*

THANKFUL

WEEK 1 • WEDNESDAY

*Write three things you are thankful for today
and why each one brings you joy.*

ONE

TWO

THREE

WEEK 1
Thursday

READ

Psalm 137

By the rivers of Babylon we sit down and weep when we remember Zion. 2 On the poplars in her midst we hang our harps, 3 for there our captors ask us to compose songs; those who mock us demand that we be happy, saying: "Sing for us a song about Zion!" 4 How can we sing a song to the Lord in a foreign land? 5 If I forget you, O Jerusalem, may my right hand be crippled. 6 May my tongue stick to the roof of my mouth, if I do not remember you, and do not give Jerusalem priority over whatever gives me the most joy. 7 Remember, O Lord, what the Edomites did on the day Jerusalem fell. They said, "Tear it down, tear it down, right to its very foundation!" 8 O daughter Babylon, soon to be devastated, how blessed will be the one who repays you for what you dished out to us. 9 How blessed will be the one who grabs your babies and smashes them on a rock.

Psalm 138
By David.

I will give you thanks with all my heart; before the heavenly assembly I will sing praises to you. 2 I will bow down toward your holy temple, and give thanks to your name, because of your loyal love and faithfulness, for you have exalted your promise above the entire sky. 3 When I cried out for help, you answered me. You made me bold and energized me. 4 Let all the kings of the earth give thanks to you, O Lord, when they hear the words you speak. 5 Let them sing about the Lord's deeds, for the Lord's splendor is magnificent. 6 Though the Lord is exalted, he looks after the lowly, and from far away humbles the proud. 7 Even when I must walk in the midst of danger, you revive me. You oppose my angry enemies, and your right hand delivers me. 8 The Lord avenges me. O Lord, your loyal love endures. Do not abandon those whom you have made.

SOAP
WEEK 1 • THURSDAY

SOAP / *Psalm 138:7–8*
SCRIPTURE / *Write out the SOAP verses*

OBSERVATION / *Write 3 - 4 observations*

APPLICATION / *Write down 1 - 2 applications*

PRAYER / *Write out a prayer over what you learned*

THANKFUL

WEEK 1 • THURSDAY

Write three things you are thankful for today and why each one brings you joy.

ONE

TWO

THREE

WEEK 1
Friday

READ

Psalm 139
For the music director, a psalm of David.

O Lord, you examine me and know me. 2 You know when I sit down and when I get up; even from far away you understand my motives. 3 You carefully observe me when I travel or when I lie down to rest; you are aware of everything I do. 4 Certainly my tongue does not frame a word without you, O Lord, being thoroughly aware of it. 5 You squeeze me in from behind and in front; you place your hand on me. 6 Your knowledge is beyond my comprehension; it is so far beyond me, I am unable to fathom it. 7 Where can I go to escape your Spirit? Where can I flee to escape your presence? 8 If I were to ascend to heaven, you would be there. If I were to sprawl out in Sheol, there you would be. 9 If I were to fly away on the wings of the dawn, and settle down on the other side of the sea, 10 even there your hand would guide me, your right hand would grab hold of me. 11 If I were to say, "Certainly the darkness will cover me, and the light will turn to night all around me," 12 even the darkness is not too dark for you to see, and the night is as bright as day; darkness and light are the same to you. 13 Certainly you made my mind and heart; you wove me together in my mother's womb. 14 I will give you thanks because your deeds are awesome and amazing. You knew me thoroughly; 15 my bones were not hidden from you, when I was made in secret and sewed together in the depths of the earth. 16 Your eyes saw me when I was inside the womb. All the days ordained for me were recorded in your scroll before one of them came into existence. 17 How difficult it is for me to fathom your thoughts about me, O God! How vast is their sum total. 18 If I tried to count them, they would outnumber the grains of sand. Even if I finished counting them, I would still have to contend with you. 19 If only you would kill the wicked, O God! Get away from me, you violent men! 20 They rebel against you and act deceitfully; your enemies lie. 21 O Lord, do I not hate those who hate you, and despise those who oppose you? 22 I absolutely hate them; they have become my enemies. 23 Examine me, O God, and probe my thoughts. Test me, and know my concerns. 24 See if there is any idolatrous way in me, and lead me in the everlasting way.

WEEK 1
Friday

Psalm 140

140 For the music director, a psalm of David. O Lord, rescue me from wicked men. Protect me from violent men, 2 who plan ways to harm me. All day long they stir up conflict. 3 Their tongues wound like a serpent; a viper's venom is behind their lips. (Selah) 4 O Lord, shelter me from the power of the wicked. Protect me from violent men, who plan to knock me over. 5 Proud men hide a snare for me; evil men spread a net by the path. They set traps for me. (Selah) 6 I say to the Lord, "You are my God." O Lord, pay attention to my plea for mercy. 7 O Sovereign Lord, my strong deliverer, you shield my head in the day of battle. 8 O Lord, do not let the wicked have their way. Do not allow their plan to succeed when they attack. (Selah) 9 As for the heads of those who surround me— may the harm done by their lips overwhelm them. 10 May he rain down fiery coals upon them. May he throw them into the fire. From bottomless pits they will not escape. 11 A slanderer will not endure on the earth; calamity will hunt down a violent man and strike him down. 12 I know that the Lord defends the cause of the oppressed and vindicates the poor. 13 Certainly the godly will give thanks to your name; the morally upright will live in your presence.

"You can never lose what you have offered to Christ."

Elisabeth Elliot

SOAP

WEEK 1 • FRIDAY

SOAP / *Psalm 139:23–34*
SCRIPTURE / *Write out the SOAP verses*

OBSERVATION / *Write 3 - 4 observations*

APPLICATION / *Write down 1 - 2 applications*

PRAYER / *Write out a prayer over what you learned*

THANKFUL

WEEK 1 · FRIDAY

*Write three things you are thankful for today
and why each one brings you joy.*

ONE

TWO

THREE

REFLECT

Record an application you learned from your SOAP study this week and how you will practically implement it in your life.

JOURNAL
your thoughts

JOURNAL
your thoughts

BRIDGE / WEEK 2

The Lord is (near) all who cry out to him, all who cry out to him *sincerely*. He satisfies the desire of his *loyal followers;* he hears their cry for help and *delivers* them.

Psalm 145:18-19

PRAY

Write down your prayer requests and praises for this week.

WEEK 2
Monday

READ

Psalm 141
A psalm of David.

O Lord, I cry out to you. Come quickly to me. Pay attention to me when I cry out to you. 2 May you accept my prayer like incense, my uplifted hands like the evening offering. 3 O Lord, place a guard on my mouth. Protect the opening of my lips. 4 Do not let me have evil desires, or participate in sinful activities with men who behave wickedly. I will not eat their delicacies. 5 May the godly strike me in love and correct me. May my head not refuse choice oil. Indeed, my prayer is a witness against their evil deeds. 6 They will be thrown over the side of a cliff by their judges. They will listen to my words, for they are pleasant. 7 As when one plows and breaks up the soil, so our bones are scattered at the mouth of Sheol. 8 Surely I am looking to you, O Sovereign Lord. In you I take shelter. Do not expose me to danger. 9 Protect me from the snare they have laid for me, and the traps the evildoers have set. 10 Let the wicked fall into their own nets, while I escape.

Psalm 142
A well-written song by David, when
he was in the cave; a prayer.

To the Lord I cry out; to the Lord I plead for mercy. 2 I pour out my lament before him; I tell him about my troubles. 3 Even when my strength leaves me, you watch my footsteps. In the path where I walk they have hidden a trap for me. 4 Look to the right and see. No one cares about me. I have nowhere to run; no one is concerned about my life. 5 I cry out to you, O Lord; I say, "You are my shelter, my security in the land of the living." 6 Listen to my cry for help, for I am in serious trouble. Rescue me from those who chase me, for they are stronger than I am. 7 Free me from prison, that I may give thanks to your name. Because of me the godly will assemble, for you will vindicate me.

SOAP
WEEK 2 · MONDAY

SOAP / *Psalm 141:3-4*
SCRIPTURE / *Write out the SOAP verses*

OBSERVATION / *Write 3 - 4 observations*

APPLICATION / *Write down 1 - 2 applications*

PRAYER / *Write out a prayer over what you learned*

THANKFUL

WEEK 2 • MONDAY

Write three things you are thankful for today and why each one brings you joy.

ONE

....
....
....
....
....
....
....

TWO

....
....
....
....
....
....
....

THREE

....
....
....
....
....
....
....

WEEK 2
Tuesday

READ

Psalm 143
A psalm of David.

O LORD, hear my prayer. Pay attention to my plea for help. Because of your faithfulness and justice, answer me. 2 Do not sit in judgment on your servant, for no one alive is innocent before you. 3 Certainly my enemies chase me. They smash me into the ground. They force me to live in dark regions, like those who have been dead for ages. 4 My strength leaves me; I am absolutely shocked. 5 I recall the old days. I meditate on all you have done; I reflect on your accomplishments. 6 I spread my hands out to you in prayer; my soul thirsts for you in a parched land. (Selah) 7 Answer me quickly, LORD. My strength is fading. Do not reject me, or I will join those descending into the grave. 8 May I hear about your loyal love in the morning, for I trust in you. Show me the way I should go, because I long for you. 9 Rescue me from my enemies, O LORD. I run to you for protection. 10 Teach me to do what pleases you, for you are my God. May your kind presence lead me into a level land. 11 O LORD, for the sake of your reputation, revive me. Because of your justice, rescue me from trouble. 12 As a demonstration of your loyal love, destroy my enemies. Annihilate all who threaten my life, for I am your servant.

WEEK 2
Tuesday

Psalm 144
By David.

The Lord, my Protector, deserves praise— the one who trains my hands for battle, and my fingers for war, 2 who loves me and is my stronghold, my refuge and my deliverer, my shield and the one in whom I take shelter, who makes nations submit to me. 3 O Lord, of what importance is the human race, that you should notice them? Of what importance is mankind, that you should be concerned about them? 4 People are like a vapor, their days like a shadow that disappears. 5 O Lord, make the sky sink and come down. Touch the mountains and make them smolder. 6 Hurl lightning bolts and scatter the enemy. Shoot your arrows and rout them. 7 Reach down from above. Grab me and rescue me from the surging water, from the power of foreigners, 8 who speak lies, and make false promises. 9 O God, I will sing a new song to you. Accompanied by a ten-stringed instrument, I will sing praises to you, 10 the one who delivers kings, and rescued David his servant from a deadly sword. 11 Grab me and rescue me from the power of foreigners, who speak lies, and make false promises. 12 Then our sons will be like plants, that quickly grow to full size. Our daughters will be like corner pillars, carved like those in a palace. 13 Our storehouses will be full, providing all kinds of food. Our sheep will multiply by the thousands and fill our pastures. 14 Our cattle will be weighted down with produce. No one will break through our walls, no one will be taken captive, and there will be no terrified cries in our city squares. 15 How blessed are the people who experience these things. How blessed are the people whose God is the Lord.

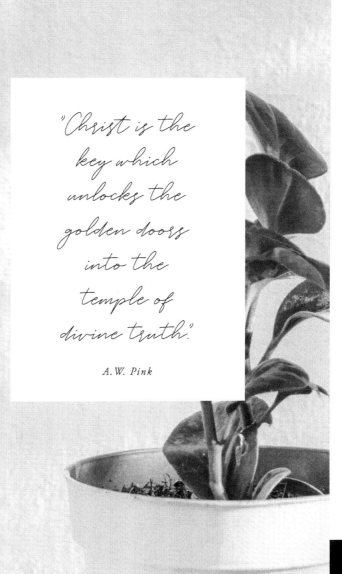

"Christ is the key which unlocks the golden doors into the temple of divine truth."

A.W. Pink

SOAP

WEEK 2 • TUESDAY

SOAP / *Psalm 144:1–2*
SCRIPTURE / *Write out the SOAP verses*

OBSERVATION / *Write 3 - 4 observations*

APPLICATION / *Write down 1 - 2 applications*

PRAYER / *Write out a prayer over what you learned*

THANKFUL

WEEK 2 • TUESDAY

Write three things you are thankful for today and why each one brings you joy.

ONE

TWO

THREE

WEEK 2
Wednesday

READ

Psalm 145
A psalm of praise; by David.

I will extol you, my God, O King. I will praise your name continually. 2 Every day I will praise you. I will praise your name continually. 3 The Lord is great and certainly worthy of praise. No one can fathom his greatness. 4 One generation will praise your deeds to another, and tell about your mighty acts. 5 I will focus on your honor and majestic splendor, and your amazing deeds. 6 They will proclaim the power of your awesome acts. I will declare your great deeds. 7 They will talk about the fame of your great kindness, and sing about your justice. 8 The Lord is merciful and compassionate; he is patient and demonstrates great loyal love. 9 The Lord is good to all, and has compassion on all he has made. 10 All your works will give thanks to you, Lord. Your loyal followers will praise you. 11 They will proclaim the splendor of your kingdom; they will tell about your power, 12 so that mankind might acknowledge your mighty acts, and the majestic splendor of your kingdom. 13 Your kingdom is an eternal kingdom, and your dominion endures through all generations. 14 The Lord supports all who fall, and lifts up all who are bent over. 15 Everything looks to you in anticipation, and you provide them with food on a regular basis. 16 You open your hand, and fill every living thing with the food it desires. 17 The Lord is just in all his actions, and exhibits love in all he does. 18 The Lord is near all who cry out to him, all who cry out to him sincerely. 19 He satisfies the desire of his loyal followers; he hears their cry for help and delivers them. 20 The Lord protects all those who love him, but he destroys all the wicked. 21 My mouth will praise the Lord. Let all who live praise his holy name forever.

Psalm 146

Praise the Lord. Praise the Lord, O my soul. 2 I will praise the Lord as long as I live. I will sing praises to my God as long as I exist. 3 Do not trust in princes, or in human beings, who cannot deliver. 4 Their life's breath departs, they return to the ground. On that day their plans die. 5 How blessed is the one whose helper is the God of Jacob, whose hope is in the Lord his God, 6 the one who made heaven and earth, the sea, and all that is in them, who remains forever faithful, 7 vindicates the oppressed, and gives food to the hungry. The Lord releases the imprisoned. 8 The Lord gives sight to the blind. The Lord lifts up all who are bent over. The Lord loves the godly. 9 The Lord protects the resident foreigner. He lifts up the fatherless and the widow, but he opposes the wicked. 10 The Lord rules forever, your God, O Zion, throughout the generations to come. Praise the Lord!

SOAP
WEEK 2 • WEDNESDAY

SOAP / *Psalm 145:17–21*
SCRIPTURE / *Write out the SOAP verses*

OBSERVATION / *Write 3 - 4 observations*

APPLICATION / *Write down 1 - 2 applications*

PRAYER / *Write out a prayer over what you learned*

THANKFUL

WEEK 2 • WEDNESDAY

*Write three things you are thankful for today
and why each one brings you joy.*

ONE

....
....
....
....
....
....
....

TWO

....
....
....
....
....
....
....

THREE

....
....
....
....
....
....
....

WEEK 2
Thursday

READ

Psalm 147

Praise the Lord, for it is good to sing praises to our God. Yes, praise is pleasant and appropriate. 2 The Lord rebuilds Jerusalem, and gathers the exiles of Israel. 3 He heals the brokenhearted, and bandages their wounds. 4 He counts the number of the stars; he names all of them. 5 Our Lord is great and has awesome power; there is no limit to his wisdom. 6 The Lord lifts up the oppressed, but knocks the wicked to the ground. 7 Offer to the Lord a song of thanks. Sing praises to our God to the accompaniment of a harp. 8 He covers the sky with clouds, provides the earth with rain, and causes grass to grow on the hillsides. 9 He gives food to the animals, and to the young ravens when they chirp. 10 He is not enamored with the strength of a horse, nor is he impressed by the warrior's strong legs. 11 The Lord takes delight in his faithful followers, and in those who wait for his loyal love. 12 Extol the Lord, O Jerusalem. Praise your God, O Zion. 13 For he makes the bars of your gates strong. He blesses your children within you. 14 He brings peace to your territory. He abundantly provides for you the best grain. 15 He sends his command through the earth; swiftly his order reaches its destination. 16 He sends the snow that is white like wool; he spreads the frost that is white like ashes. 17 He throws his hailstones like crumbs. Who can withstand the cold wind he sends? 18 He then orders it all to melt; he breathes on it, and the water flows. 19 He proclaims his word to Jacob, his statutes and regulations to Israel. 20 He has not done so with any other nation; they are not aware of his regulations. Praise the Lord!

Psalm 148

Praise the Lord. Praise the Lord from the sky. Praise him in the heavens. 2 Praise him, all his angels. Praise him, all his heavenly assembly. 3 Praise him, O sun and moon. Praise him, all you shiny stars. 4 Praise him, O highest heaven, and you waters above the sky. 5 Let them praise the name of the Lord, for he gave the command and they came into existence. 6 He established them so they would endure; he issued a decree that will not be revoked. 7 Praise the Lord from the earth, you sea creatures and all you ocean depths, 8 O fire and hail, snow and clouds, O stormy wind that carries out his orders, 9 you mountains and all you hills, you fruit trees and all you cedars, 10 you animals and all you cattle, you creeping things and birds, 11 you kings of the earth and all you nations, you princes and all you leaders on the earth, 12 you young men and young women, you elderly, along with you children. 13 Let them praise the name of the Lord, for his name alone is exalted; his majesty extends over the earth and sky. 14 He has made his people victorious, and given all his loyal followers reason to praise— the Israelites, the people who are close to him. Praise the Lord!

SOAP
WEEK 2 • THURSDAY

SOAP / *Psalm 147:11*
SCRIPTURE / *Write out the SOAP verses*

OBSERVATION / *Write 3 - 4 observations*

APPLICATION / *Write down 1 - 2 applications*

PRAYER / *Write out a prayer over what you learned*

THANKFUL

WEEK 2 • THURSDAY

*Write three things you are thankful for today
and why each one brings you joy.*

ONE

TWO

THREE

WEEK 2
Friday

READ

Psalm 149

Praise the Lord. Sing to the Lord a new song. Praise him in the assembly of the godly. 2 Let Israel rejoice in their Creator. Let the people of Zion delight in their King. 3 Let them praise his name with dancing. Let them sing praises to him to the accompaniment of the tambourine and harp. 4 For the Lord takes delight in his people; he exalts the oppressed by delivering them. 5 Let the godly rejoice because of their vindication. Let them shout for joy upon their beds. 6 May the praises of God be in their mouths and a two-edged sword in their hands, 7 in order to take revenge on the nations, and punish foreigners. 8 The godly bind their enemies' kings in chains, and their nobles in iron shackles, 9 and execute the judgment to which their enemies have been sentenced. All his loyal followers will be vindicated. Praise the Lord.

Psalm 150

Praise the Lord! Praise God in his sanctuary; praise him in the sky, which testifies to his strength! 2 Praise him for his mighty acts; praise him for his surpassing greatness! 3 Praise him with the blast of the horn; praise him with the lyre and the harp! 4 Praise him with the tambourine and with dancing; praise him with stringed instruments and the flute! 5 Praise him with loud cymbals; praise him with clanging cymbals! 6 Let everything that has breath praise the Lord! Praise the Lord!

SOAP

WEEK 2 • FRIDAY

SOAP / *Psalm 149:4–5*
SCRIPTURE / *Write out the SOAP verses*

OBSERVATION / *Write 3 - 4 observations*

APPLICATION / *Write down 1 - 2 applications*

PRAYER / *Write out a prayer over what you learned*

THANKFUL

WEEK 2 • FRIDAY

*Write three things you are thankful for today
and why each one brings you joy.*

ONE

TWO

THREE

REFLECT

Record an application you learned from your SOAP study this week and how you will practically implement it in your life.

JOURNAL
your thoughts

JOURNAL
your thoughts

Join Us

ONLINE
lovegodgreatly.com

JOURNALS
lovegodgreatly.com/store

FACEBOOK
lovegodgreatly

INSTAGRAM
@lovegodgreatlyofficial

APP
Love God Greatly

....

CONTACT US
info@lovegodgreatly.com

CONNECT
#LoveGodGreatly

FOR YOU

What we offer

35+ Translations
Bible Reading Plans
Online Bible Study
Love God Greatly App
Over 200 Countries Served
Bible Study Journals
Community Groups
Love God Greatly Bible
Love God Greatly Journal

Each study includes

Three Weekly Blog Posts
Daily Devotions
Memory Verses
Weekly Challenges
Weekly Reflection Questions
Bridge Reading Plan

Other studies

Faith over Perfection
In Jesus You Are...
Friendship
In the Beginning
The Gospel of Mark
Shame Breaker
Everlasting Covenant
Jesus Our Everything
Know Love
Empowered: Yesterday and Today
Risen
Draw Near
Beatitudes
Esther
Words Matter
Walking in Victory
To Do Justice, To Love Kindness, To Walk Humbly
Faithful Love
Choose Brave
Savior
Promises of God
Love the Loveless
Truth Over Lies

1 & 2 Thessalonians
Fear & Anxiety
James
His Name Is...
Philippians
1 & 2 Timothy
Sold Out
Ruth
Broken & Redeemed
Walking in Wisdom
God With Us
In Everything Give Thanks
You Are Forgiven
David
Ecclesiastes
Names of God
Galatians
Psalm 119
1st & 2nd Peter
Made For Community
The Road To Christmas
The Source Of Gratitude
You Are Loved

Made in the USA
Middletown, DE
23 October 2021